More

Illustrated History

of the

RAILWAYS

of

HULL

by

W.B.Yeadon

This edition published by:
Book Law / Railbus Publications 2006
382 Carlton Hill
Nottingham
NG4 1JA

Copyright Challenger Publications 1995
ISBN 1 899624 03 1
Printed by The Amadeus Press, Cleckheaton, BD19 4TQ
First published in the UK by Challenger Publications

PREFACE

When a previous joint work with Mick Nicholson, *An Illustrated History of Hull's Railways (Irwell Press 1993),* was published, we expected that sales would almost all be made locally, so it was a pleasant surprise indeed to learn that one had given considerable satisfaction as far away in this world as it is possible to travel. From New Zealand an expatriate enthusiast wrote expressing the hope that we would do a follow-up book. We were also cheered by the volume of British correspondence that we received, which had a congratulatory/critical ratio of at least 10 to 1, and the latter was more concerned with what we had left out than what we had put in. More attention to the pre-Grouping period would have been welcomed, as would have been more about goods traffic, so eighteen months on I have tried to take both those into account in this miscellaneous history, although lamentably, for today's goods traffic, no more than a single page would be required to describe it.

Those accustomed to dealing with publicity aver that one picture is worth anything from a hundred to a thousand words, so this book has been loaded accordingly. The last one left both of us regretting what a wealth of photographs we had been unable to include, so another bite at the cherry, albeit a solo one this time, gives me a satisfaction that I hope you will be able to share with me. I make no apologies for including yet another chapter on the swing bridges over the River Hull at Wilmington, this time with a new selection of photographs which came to light from various local sources. That leads me to pay a sincere tribute to the many people who have so willingly helped by providing photographs, and where known, the pictures have been credited suitably. I am also indebted to several railway employees, both currently serving, and retired, for providing me with invaluable first-hand information, and particularly for leads to useful further research. In that sphere, I have been amazed at the wealth of traffic data which arises from diligent digging in the Local Studies Library, but particularly with the skill and unwavering patience the staff there display at what must seem to them the most fatuous enquiries. This book owes a great deal to their invariably cheerful assistance. As a result, I too feel to know far more about Hull than I ever learned at school or at night classes.

The individuals and volunteer bodies to whom I owe a great deal, and would like to thank, are Michael Back, The Reverend David Benson, Steve Bramley, Tony Buckton, Michael Clark, Nick Fleetwood, Peter Harrod, Steve Jordan, Mike Lake, Ian K.Watson, David Smith, John Turner of 53A Models, Bert Worsfold, Crich Tramway Museum, Memory Lane of Hull, the North Eastern Railway Association, and the Signalling Record Society. Finally a big thank you to Mick who was always ready to answer any queries, especially regarding signalling matters.

Willie Yeadon, Hull, April 1995.

INDEX

PASSENGER STATIONS WITHIN HULL'S CITY BOUNDARIES

Since 1981, our only railway station is Paragon, which opened on 8th May 1848 and is now approaching its 150th anniversary; as could be expected, it has seen both ups and downs. For its first fifty years the Arrival, Middle, and Departure Platforms had to suffice, but became totally insufficient to deal with the rapidly growing traffic. During the period 1903 to 1905 extensive additions and alterations were made, resulting in there being fourteen platforms available. The main station had nos.1 to 9, all full length and under cover, no.10 was a short one, used mainly by steam railcars and also for loading express fish traffic, whilst nos.11 to 14 (with two non-platform lines between 12 and 13) to the south-west, and out in the open, catered for excursion trains.

After the additional portion was brought into use on December 12th 1904, work began on replacing the roof of the 1848 station. About two-thirds of the old roof had been taken down when, about 9.30 a.m. on Saturday 7th January 1905, the remainder collapsed with the disastrous result shown in our picture. Six men working on the roof were thrown down about 25 feet with it, and two engaged at ground level were partially buried. Prompt rescue and transport to the nearby Infirmary found that, incredibly, the injuries were limited to one broken arm, one broken leg, various cuts, bruises, and shock. A steam crane driver removing platform flagstones was knocked off the crane which finished up buried under broken glass, wood, and ironwork. He got away with the broken forearm, and the temporary loss of his coat and tobacco pouch!; he was however able to give a coherent account to newspaper reporters.

Apart from the additions to the station and permanent way, complete resignalling was also called for. Both Park Street and Paragon signalboxes were replaced and the opportunity was taken to install the Westinghouse electro-pneumatic system into the new signalboxes and all points and signals were power worked. Even in those far-off and labour intensive days, such a scheme could not be carried out overnight and it was to be 3rd July 1905 before the resignalling became fully operative. Those signals served until replaced by the colour-light signalling with O.C.S. route setting, which became effective on 24th April 1938.

Inevitably, some rough followed all these smoothing improvements. 5th February 1927 saw two incoming trains have a side-long collision between Argyle and Park Street bridges. Casualties were fortunately limited to three slight injuries to people, but loco-wise right triumphed over might. The small LNER 0-4-4 tank engine which was running correctly to the signals, toppled the twice as big LMS 4-6-0 tender engine which had over-run its signal. But real tragedy struck only nine days later and at almost the same location. A head-on collision of two passenger trains caused 12 deaths and 24 serious injuries, also both engines having to be scrapped. Then events proceeded as normal (apart from a day's disorganised chaos when route-setting was introduced in April 1938) until the German Air Force blitzed us on two consecutive nights in May 1941. The large department store opposite the front of the station was completely destroyed, as was the Corporation's main bus garage adjacent to the north side of the station. Paragon station was itself showered

with incendiary bombs, but heroic efforts by its staff limited the resultant fires to one small corner. Sadly, that happened to be where in 1933, the Corporation and the LNER had established a small museum of local railway artefacts, so we were deprived of some irreplaceable items. On those two nights alone, 420 Hull people were killed, and another 325 seriously injured, but Paragon's luck otherwise held out through the six years of war and no less than 82 air raids during which bombs were dropped. Even on the day after the blitz I arrived in the 8.25 a.m. from Leeds and returned by the 5.05 p.m. from Paragon, and both trains ran exactly to time.

The post-war rebuilding of the devastated city was planned by a Prof.Abercrombie, and included in his ideas was abolition of the rail/road crossings. He proposed complete closure of Paragon station, and by making use of the high-level ex Hull & Barnsley line, its replacement by a big new station in the Cannon Street area. Paragon was spared that fate because those who had the powers to implement his scheme did not have the vast sum of money needed for it. About twenty years later, a certain Dr. Beeching helped to close many of the level crossings by simply axing the railway lines concerned, which drastically reduced the train service at Paragon station. Today, only seven platforms are used, or needed. Those which were known for the last ninety years as platforms 9 to 3 have been renumbered in reverse order as nos.1 to 7. Now there are often times during the day when it is almost as quiet as a cathedral, to the great sorrow of railway enthusiasts such as your author.

Paragon however is by no means the only station Hull has had. At the 1994 annual exhibition of the Hull Miniature Railway Society, the local newspaper ran a competition inviting entrants to name at least twelve railway stations which had been open in Hull, since our railways started in 1840. The real railway buffs had plenty of scope, because there have been eighteen, plus a couple which were just halts. First was Manor House Street station, used from July 1840 to May 1848, and again from May 1853 until November 1854. From 1848 it was superseded by the more centrally situated Paragon Street station, and its 1853/4 re-opening was in an attempt to run a suburban passenger service on the Victoria Dock branch to the terminus station of that name, which the Hull & Holderness Railway opened in May 1853 on the south side of Hedon Road. Where the York & North Midland's line from Manor House

(left) **A postcard view of the 7th January 1905 roof disaster at Paragon.** *Authors collection.*

(left) **Views of the old Paragon station are relatively rare. This view shows, in the centre middle ground, what is believed to be the old Park Street signal box of 1875 vintage. The location of the bracket signal suggests that the picture was taken during the rebuilding of the station in 1903/4.** *Memory Lane, Hull.*

The opening of the Hull & Barnsley Railway in July 1885 added three to the city's stations. Its original intention was to have its terminus in Kingston Square, near to the city centre, but that plan was thwarted by the high cost of the property it would have to demolish to get there, so it had to be content with one on Cannon Street. Just to the east of where the line bridged Beverley Road, it split, that for the heavy goods going straight on to Alexandra Dock, whilst that for passenger, parcels and fruit traffic branched to the right. On the branch, but close to the junction, and at the end of Fitzroy Street, their Beverley Road Station was opened; definitely an upstairs/downstairs building with the platform at the upper level. Both Cannon Street and Beverley Road stations were closed after the last train had used them on Sunday 13th July 1924, because their passenger trains were then able to be diverted to use Paragon station. The third Hull & Barnsley station was the emigrant station (with Customs House) erected on Alexandra Dock at the western end. It was busiest in the years 1890 to 1905 with those who were leaving Europe to make a new life in the United States of America, but not all of them travelled on to Liverpool to face the rigours of another sea voyage in what was then the steerage class conditions. Some are known to have settled in Hull, with their descendants now being Hull citizens. The 1914-18 war completely and quickly put an end to that traffic, so Alexandra Dock station closed and was reopened subsequently only in 1919 as a temporary measure to repatriate German P.O.W's from the war of 1914-18.

In 1899, that part of the railway line between Hessle Road and Cottingham South signalboxes was changed from its original 1845 single, to double track, and where it crossed Anlaby Road at Newington on the level, a pair of platforms, 246 and 231 yards long were constructed. They were mainly for use when agricultural shows were held on adjacent land, the prestige Yorkshire Show being held there in 1899, and again in 1905. By the time of the latter, electric tramcars running along Anlaby Road could handle passengers visiting the Show, so Newington station was closed in March 1906.

Finally, on 6th January 1951, Boothferry Park station was opened especially to deal with football match traffic for Hull City A.F.C.'s home matches. As of April 1995, it has not yet been closed officially, but it has now not been used for many years. Other than the single platform

crossed both Hessle, and Anlaby roads, on the level, trains halted for passengers, but no platforms were provided at either, so can only be classed as the two halts. The crossings at Spring Bank, Beverley Road, Wincolmlee, and Holderness Road (also all on the level) fared better because they each got platforms and conventional station buildings. The one at Spring Bank was first named Cemetery, from 1866 as Cemetery Gates, and from November 1881 as Botanic Gardens. Whilst the cemetery is still open to visitors, the gardens only survived to 1890, and by 1893 Hymers College had been opened there. The other three stations were named respectively Stepney, Sculcoates, and Southcoates, and both the latter were moved to other sites subsequently. In 1894 Southcoates moved further east, and to the opposite side of the track to avoid the Withernsea service conflicting with the increasing traffic to and from Victoria Dock. In June 1912 Sculcoates was closed and replaced by Wilmington, near to where the line bridged Cleveland Street. That station had hitherto been further east, where the Hull & Hornsea Railway had opened its station at the junction it made with the Victoria Dock branch. When the North Eastern Railway was able to divert the Withernsea trains into using Paragon station in June 1864, the Victoria Dock terminus station was then closed. The other four, Botanic Gardens, Stepney, Wilmington, and Southcoates were all Beeching victims and were closed on 19th October 1964. There were two more closures on that same day; Marfleet, which the Hull & Holderness had opened on 27th June 1854, and was not affected by the diversion of the Withernsea trains to Paragon ten years later, the other being Sutton-

on-Hull on the Hornsea branch. Until December 1874 its name was simply Sutton, and it did not qualify for our consideration until 1929 when the Hull city boundaries were extended to take in Sutton village.

Certainly a railway station having full facilities but never any trains, was the one named Corporation Pier, opened in March 1849 by the Manchester, Sheffield & Lincolnshire Railway which served the railway-owned ferry across the River Humber to the rail head at New Holland. The name of a station lacking trains often turns up in quiz programmes, but here, there is really nothing unusual about it, because we still have an Admiral who does not have any ships (our Lord Mayor is Admiral of the Humber, and receives the appropriate naval courtesies from all visiting warships) and also a Bishop who does not have a cathedral. The opening of the road bridge across the Humber in July 1981 ended the ferry and brought closure to Corporation Pier station.

Another station entirely associated with ships was Riverside Quay, opened 11th May 1907 and closed in September 1939 with the cessation of the steamer services to the continent. The 1939 war put a very definite end not only to those trains, but also to the station buildings, because they were completely destroyed by German bombs in the May 1941 blitz.

The site, and tracks of Riverside Quay station did however rise from the ashes, for starting on 16th August 1946, they served as the transfer point from ship to rail for the troops coming on home leave from Germany, and less happily, for those whose leave had expired. Three specials, to London, Manchester, and Edinburgh distributed each ship's 1400 passengers.

and the inclined walkway to the entrance to the ground, it has no facilities, nor has it appeared in official timetables, so it and also Newington, should more properly be regarded as halts rather than as stations. The line on which Boothferry Park stands was part of the line to the Hull & Barnsley's large goods station at Neptune Street, and that football station was served directly from (and back to) Paragon station. When large numbers of 'away' supporters were due to arrive in Hull on Football Specials, it was convenient, after the 1962 resignalling, to route them from Hessle Road junction directly to Boothferry Park station, thus saving them the trek along Anlaby Road from Paragon, and also relieving local inhabitants from any probable hassle from their exuberance.

With our account being deliberately restricted to stations inside the Hull city boundary, we have reluctantly to discard another regularly used, and timetabled, halt because it was just a quarter of a mile outside the boundary. That was Springhead Halt, situated where the original Hull & Barnsley line bridged Wolfreton Lane, and served by the trains (and Sentinel railcars) between Hull and South Howden. Opened as a single platform made of wood, on 8th April 1929, six trains a day in each direction, to set down only, were still calling there at the end of the LNER, but it closed completely on 1st August 1955.

(above) **North Eastern Railway F class (LNER Class D22) No.808 departs Paragon with an express about 1922. Typical of the express passenger motive power working from Hull at the time, these engines were superseded by the more powerful Gresley D49 4-4-0s.** *T.G.Hepburn.*

(below) **Enemy air raids on Hull throughout the last war were regular, devastating and disruptive. This July 1941 scene shows the result of one such raid when a bomb exploded on the coal sidings just north of Paragon station. The rolling stock on the right seems to have suffered damage whilst in the centre background a 3-tank gas wagon is surrounded by hastily scribed 'No Smoking' notices. Workmen make good the ramp to the coal staithes on the left whilst the linesmen struggle to untangle nearly a hundred fallen line wires.** *Authors collection.*

An unidentified B1 4-6-0 takes water at the end of Paragon's platform 12, on Wednesday 18th April 1962, before departing with a parcels train. The driver stands waiting to turn off the water supply. Despite being dressed in the regulation overalls of that era, the driver is neatly attired with a white shirt and blue tie, a reflection of the pride and dignity of his calling. *Ian K.Watson.*

Shortly after transfer to Botanic shed in October 1954 ex-LMS Fowler 2-6-2T 40061 is seen running into Paragon station. The motor-fitted locomotive still carries its 26F Lees (Oldham) shedplate. *N.E.Stead.*

An empty, two-car Class 101 d.m.u. stands in platform 9 at Paragon awaiting its next call of duty on 22nd July 1984. This was to be the last summer of the old station layout and work had already started on the remodelling and resignalling which was to culminate in the station as we know it today. Under the new order platform 9 became platform 2. *53A Models, Hull.*

Paragon station Sunday 7th August 1988. The station is but a shadow of its not-so-long-ago better days. Six platforms on the north side of the station have been taken out of use, the North Carriage Sidings have gone and the choice of destination for passengers is limited compared with say, the 1960's. The new order in the shape of a Class 150/2 Sprinter diesel multiple unit is running into the current No.2 platform whilst a not so young Class 50 diesel locomotive named ILLUSTRIOUS, in Network South East livery, stables after having worked in on a railtour. *Steve Jordan.*

A deserted Paragon station on Sunday 20th January 1991. 47413 stands in platform 7 after working in from King's Cross. At this date the King's Cross - Hull was the only regular locomotive hauled passenger train in the area; today our few remaining London trains are operated as an HST service. *Tony Buckton.*

To Hornsea

To Botanic Gardens engine shed

West Parade Jct

Victoria Crossing

To Scarborough

Signal Box

Cottages

Argyle Street Bridge

Signal Box

Cottages

To Anlaby Road Jct

To Anlaby Road Jct

N

A

B

Park Street
Signal Box

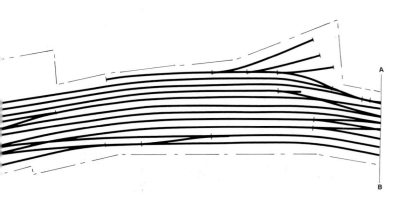

PARAGON STATION
& APPROACHES 1933

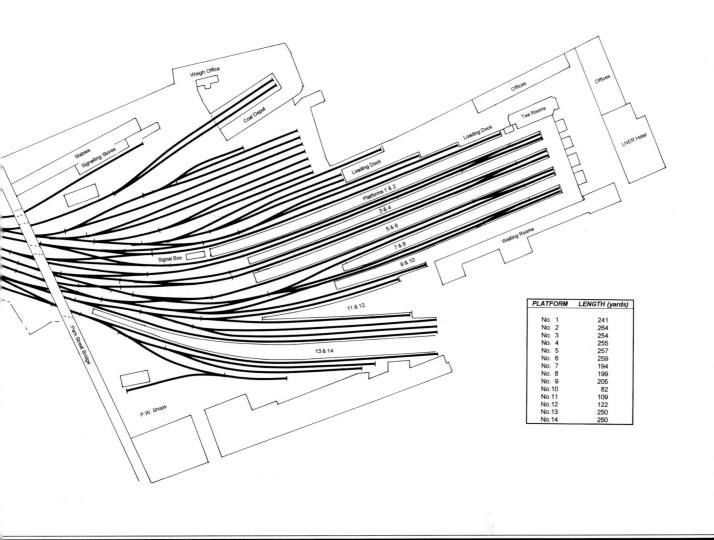

PLATFORM	LENGTH (yards)
No. 1	241
No. 2	264
No. 3	254
No. 4	255
No. 5	257
No. 6	259
No. 7	194
No. 8	199
No. 9	205
No.10	82
No.11	109
No.12	122
No.13	250
No.14	250

Hardly inspiring to any would be traveller. This was the timber clad frontage of the H&BR Cannon Street terminus in July 1924, the month of closure. *Authors collection.*

(left) Although the photograph is of a somewhat dubious quality, it is worth including to show what was the last passenger train to leave Cannon Street station, the 10.40 a.m. to Cudworth and Sheffield. The locomotive is D24 no.2428 built for the H&B in 1910 by Kitson & Co. as Class J. The five members of the class survived until 1933/4, working mainly from Paragon to Doncaster and York. *H.Monkman.*

(bottom) It was the original intention of the H&BR to have the Hull terminus of their railway in Kingston Square, and later still in Charlotte Street. Then during 1884 owing to the severe financial restraints of the company it was decided to hastily adapt the Cannon Street carriage shed and sidings to serve as the terminus. Being away from the business area Cannon Street did to some extent hamper passenger traffic. Conversely a large amount of both general merchandise, and domestic coal was handled, and to deal with this traffic, reasonably extensive sidings were provided on both sides of the railway. Although passenger trains ceased running on 13th July 1924 the station remained in use as a goods depot for another 44 years, and was not finally closed until 3rd June 1968. There were only three platforms, and platform No.1 features prominently in this circa 1948 photograph, alongside is the former Down Main line, whilst the lines to the left were once the carriage sidings. Just to the left of centre is the locomotive water tank, and this complete with its wooden legs is quite reminiscent of American practice and the "Wild West". Seen through the bar of the loading gauge is the boarded up and long out of use signal box. *C. T. Goode.*

STORE at CANNON STREET GOODS STATION, HULL.

PEEK FREAN & COMPANY, LIMITED.

Scale : 30' 0" to 1 inch.

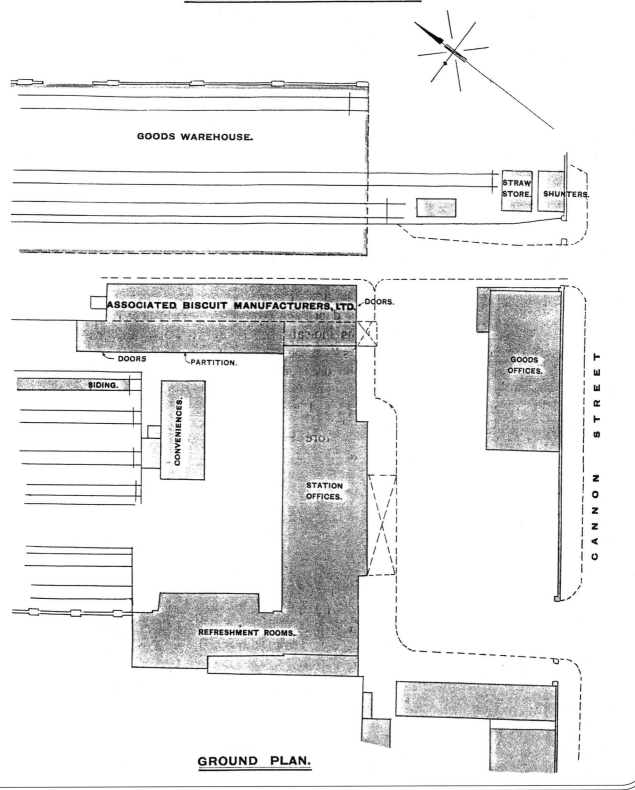

GOODS WAREHOUSE.

STRAW STORE.

SHUNTERS.

ASSOCIATED BISCUIT MANUFACTURERS, LTD.

DOORS.

DOORS.

PARTITION.

SIDING.

CONVENIENCES.

STATION OFFICES.

GOODS OFFICES.

CANNON STREET

REFRESHMENT ROOMS.

GROUND PLAN.

The H&B Cannon Street goods shed in 1969 used by a local timber company. The design of the building, with its west side open to the elements, was obviously influenced by the optimism of the 1880's when possible expansion westwards was envisaged as the railway became more established in Hull. Sadly the Cannon Street goods facilities were, like the passenger facilities, underused but lasted a good while longer. *Authors collection.*

(left) The brick built offices of the Cannon Street goods depot in 1969. Parts of the Cannon Street complex had been rented to various private companies from 1927 (see previous page) and when BR left the depot in 1968 it continued to house local traders until demolished. *Authors collection.*

(below) A plan of Beverley Road Station in 1910. Closed when passenger services were withdrawn from Cannon Street in 1924, the station stood for many years in a derelict condition. *Crown copyright reserved.*

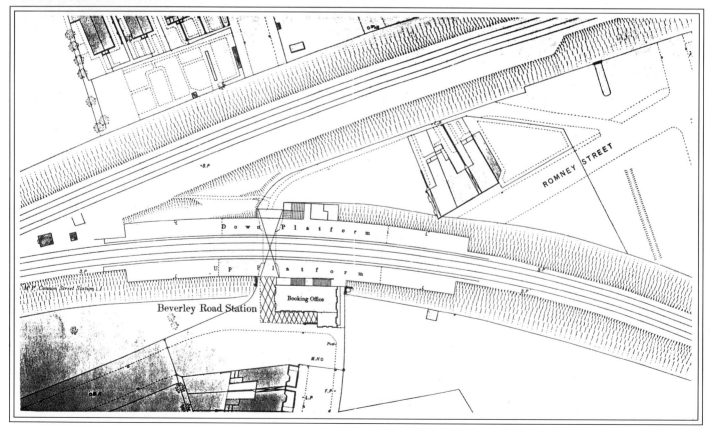

Stepney station in 1964, the year of its closure. The wonderful architecture of the station house is apparent. Although the line to Wilmington and beyond was converted to colour light signalling in the early 1960's, the station illumination was still by gas light. *Mowat collection.*

An Edwardian view of a returning excursion train on the Up Line passing through Botanic Gardens Station hauled by a 0-6-0 tender engine no.606, which survived to July 1926 in LNER class J22. Several typical enamel advertisements of the period are displayed along the down platform fence, also behind this and out of sight are the coal sidings. The same fence also forms a convenient fixing for the usual spartan platform illumination, in this case by gas, and for which the supply pipes can be seen not too firmly clipped to the fence boards. Other details are the standard NER platform seat of composite cast iron and wood construction, while the telegraph pole with its short line arms is another typical feature of the period. To quote round figures, and now ninety years on, the train would be about to pass through the bar of the Old Zoological public house.
Memory Lane Hull.

The railway first came to the village of Sutton (to use the abbreviated but incorrect title) on 28th March 1864, when the Hull & Hornsea Railway opened. This was single line throughout its 13 miles, and commenced from a junction with the Hull & Holderness Railway at Wilmington. The entire branch was eventually converted to double line, in a somewhat piecemeal manner, and probably commenced at Hornsea in July 1898. By 1904 the complete branch had been re-laid as a double line of railway, the portion between Sutton and Swine being ready by late 1902. In this picture we are looking off the road bridge and in the Down direction or north-eastwards towards Hornsea. The rural nature of the area is self evident, as is also the primitive construction of the two station buildings, both little more then wooden huts. Owing to the nature of the 1902 alterations it was necessary to provide new Up and Down platforms, the original single line then becoming the Down line. The work was done in this way to save the expense of extending or replacing the original road bridge, which had been manufactured by Messrs Close, Ayre & Nicholson, of Phoenix Foundry, York in 1863. Sutton became an unstaffed halt on 4th January 1960. *Authors collection.*

The aftermath of the air raids of 14th July 1943. About that time the railways in the Southcoates area received more than their fair share of attention from enemy bombers. Apart from the bomb crater which the men are busily engaged in filling, and the obvious breach in the Up Withernsea line there seems to have been very little other damage. As one may expect there is not a youthful face among the platelayers, not surprisingly as all the young men were away. Note the whitewashed platform edge to help in blackout hours.
Ian Scotney collection.

As mentioned elsewhere on Saturday 10th October 1964 the Railway Correspondence & Travel Society organised a railtour which covered most of Hull's then extensive rail system. This view of Southcoates station looking north - west is a product of that tour, the train is on the normally goods only No.2 Reception or Angle Road, the other lines are from left to right, No.1 Reception or Angle Road, Up Main, Down Main, and finally, full of loaded timber wagons, Coal Sidings, and "Soccy Yard". Southcoates by the way was one of the relatively few NER stations to have an island platform, but coincidentally Wilmington the next station along the line, and following its 1912 rebuilding, also had a single island platform. *Ian K Watson.*

Another mid 1960s view of Southcoates. By this date the passenger trains had ceased, but as the well polished rails show, there was still plenty of general goods and transfer traffic. Derelict to the right are the remains of the one time gateman's hut, both it and its occupant had become redundant in the early 60s when the 'Wig Wag' road traffic lights were installed. The signal is an interesting mix of the two sizes of bracket that comprised the standard NE Region 'Plate and Angle' signal, the left hand doll complete with its miniature arm is located on a 3ft 6in bracket, whilst its right hand counterpart is of the more usual 6ft 0ins construction. Here we are looking at the back of the signal, but in the direction of traffic the arms are from left to right, No.9 Down Main to Coal Sidings, No.3 Down Main Inner Home, and No.10 Down Main to Up Receptions or Goods Roads signals. Today most if not all of this view, in the name of progress, has been swept away, and we doubt if many of today's motorists driving along Mount Pleasant will even realise it was once a railway. *Ian K Watson.*

The paddle steamer TATTERSHALL CASTLE sets out from New Holland to Corporation Pier, Hull in the early afternoon of 10th May 1946. The ferry service across the Humber was started by the M S & L R in 1848 and continued to ply back and forth across the river until the opening of the Humber bridge in 1981. The 'station' at Corporation Pier was opened in 1849 and never saw a train. *H.C.Casserley.*

VARIOUS SNIPPETS ON HULL'S PASSENGER TRAFFIC

The railway in Hull has catered for passenger traffic for more than 150 years, starting in July 1840 with Manor House Street station providing a service to Selby, and thence on to Leeds. It was soon recognised that rail could give easy access to the coast, Bridlington being reached by 1846, with the link to Scarborough in October 1847, followed in 1854 by the line to Withernsea, and then in 1864 to Hornsea. Hull folk regarded the latter pair as particularly their own for giving them the chance to get some fresh sea air. Despite the swing to motor transport, and those two being within cycling distance, it is interesting to note the extent to which Hull people still went by rail to Withernsea and Hornsea as late as 1957, only seven years before those lines fell to the Beeching axe. The weekend of 15th and 16th June was in the middle of a heat wave, which sparked an urge to get to the seaside. On the Sunday, between 9.00 a.m. and 1.00 p.m. 11,000 passengers left Paragon station, all eight booking office windows needed to deal with them, those for other destinations being diverted to the Enquiry Office to get their tickets. At one period a queue of 3,000 encircled the station. The suburban stations at Botanic Gardens, and at Stepney booked another 5,500 to Hornsea and to Withernsea, whilst 2,000 more for the latter joined already well-filled trains at Marfleet. British Railways was then capable of dealing with such abnormalities, and willing to do so. In addition to running the full summer train service, engines, carriages, and staff were found to run ten extra trains. In the evening, a 20-minute service operated on both branches until about 10.30 p.m. to get people home. Those were the days when you were *NOT* asked 'Is your journey really necessary?'

In the 1930's the railway really offered friendly facilities, and on Saturdays from 5.00 p.m. they ran 'Evening Excursions'. To Hornsea and to Withernsea they were 'express' for which the fare was one shilling and three old pennies (less than 6½ p). Similarly, to Bridlington it was one and sixpence (7½p), and they took you the 103½ miles to Leeds and back for two shillings - 10p in today's money. In most of those years your author organised a works annual trip to Leeds Grand Theatre pantomime, and because there were always more than 50 in the party, they were granted reserved compartments without any extra charge. Leaving Hull at 5.00 p.m., they were into Leeds station by 6.30, and return at 11.00 p.m. got them into Paragon about 12.30 a.m. Sunday morning, where the Corporation obliged with special buses on all main routes at a fare of fourpence. Similar facilities enabled you to have a full evening's dancing at Bridlington's Spa Ballroom with no risk of it being spoiled by a tortuous road trip home.

WHAT WAS THE LONGEST REGULAR JOURNEY YOU COULD MAKE FROM HULL?

It has been interesting to research how far you could go in a train starting from Hull without having to change trains. The quick answer would be the 196 miles to London, but that distance could be almost doubled. In the 1939 summer timetable you could leave Paragon at 10.45 a.m. and relax for the 362 miles to Swansea, reached at 8.45 p.m. with restaurant car facilities from Sheffield to Swansea. The return service was even quicker, and that pair of trains had the unofficial title of 'Ports-to-Ports'. Its main users for the full distance were the crews of ships moving from South Wales ports to Hull, or to Newcastle and vice versa. The main train started from Newcastle, the Hull coaches being attached (and detached) at Sheffield's Victoria station.

In recent years the Trans-Pennine diesel trains ran the 218 miles to Holyhead, and we also had a through service to Brighton of about 250 miles, which was handy for those using Gatwick airport. On September 10th 1977, admittedly on an excursion, but publicly advertised, the author had the enthusiast's appreciation of through travel to and from Margate, hauled both ways by diesel locomotive 47180 brought specially from Immingham shed to do that unusual trip. Definitely very much a 'one-off', it really does not count in this context, but is surely worth mentioning. The furthest that you can currently travel is the 256 miles to Edinburgh on one of the occasional 'Shoppers Trips' which are organised by local charities, and travel firms. So, the 362 miles to, and also from, Swansea as a regular time-tabled working still holds the record - unless you know better.

Standing at the Stepney down platform signals, L1 2-6-4T 67766 blows off whilst waiting for the road to Hornsea or Withernsea. At the time of this picture the old NER was still very much in evidence; the clerestory coach (which was probably still gas lit) was a NER product as was the two-doll bracket signal. This signal was brought into use 22nd March 1903, the same day as the new facing connection to the Down Goods Independent was installed. A month later on Monday 22nd April these new points along with the miniature arm signal, as shown here, was brought into use. Notice also the telegraph wires are bound into one cable for crossing the highway; this had been necessary for the coming of the electric trams and had been carried out as long ago as 9th December 1900. *N.E.Stead.*

This shot is possibly reproduced from an old post-card and suggests the early Edwardian period. The view post-dates the building of Botanic Gardens engine shed, the give away being the five runs of point rodding visible to the bottom right of the picture. A further detail to note is the engine shed siding which at this date had not been extended eastwards to the level crossing, this in a later picture would figure quite prominently to the left of the Up main line. The engine is No.955 an 0-4-4T of NER class B.T.P (Bogie Tank Passenger), and will in all certainty be allocated to Botanic Gardens shed. The train which can be no other than one bound for Hornsea or Withernsea is on the Down main line and is passing over the junction with the Victoria Dock Goods lines. No.955 was the only one of its class of 124 to be fitted with this style of cab, and brass cap on its chimney, so altered in May 1902.
Memory Lane Hull.

Even Springhead's goods engines were pressed into passenger service during the summer season. Here J28 no.2412, an ex H&B Class L1, has charge of a Withernsea Express, one of the Evening Excursions in the 1932-37 years.
Authors collection.

A Trans-Pennine unit departs Hull for Liverpool in 1967 and is passing the carriage washing plant.
The Rev.J.D.Benson.

WEEKDAY DEPARTURES FROM PARAGON STATION (16th September 1957 to 8th June 1958)

AM	TO
4.38	Brough, Goole, Thorne (North), Stainforth & Hatfield
5.30	Arram, Driffield, Bridlington, Bempton, Hunmanby, Filey, Seamer, Scarborough
5.30	Leeds (City) and intermediate stations (except Broomfleet, Staddlethorpe, South Eastrington, Wressle)
5.40	Cottingham, Beverley
5.55	Bridlington and intermediate stations (except Arram)
6.10	Doncaster and intermediate stations; Sheffield (Victoria)
6.38	Brough, Goole
6.40	Botanic Gardens, Hedon, Ryehill & Burstwick, Keyingham, Ottringham, Patrington, Withernsea
6.44	Goole and intermediate stations
6.55	York and intermediate stations (except Cherry Burton, Kipling Cotes, Warthill)
6.58	Hornsea and intermediate stations (except Sigglesthorne)
7.00	Brough, South Eastrington, North Howden, Wressle, Hemingbrough, Selby and intermediate stations to Leeds (City)
7.10	Cottingham, Beverley
7.15	Withernsea and intermediate stations
7.22	Doncaster and intermediate stations
7.42	Hornsea and intermediate stations (except Sutton-on-Hull, Swine, Whitedale)
7.44	Scarborough and intermediate stations
7.50	Leeds (City) and intermediate stations (except Hambleton, Garforth, Osmondthorpe, Marsh Lane)
7.50	Cottingham, Beverley, Market Weighton, Pocklington, York
8.05	Doncaster and intermediate stations
8.05	Cottingham, Beverley
8.25	Hessle, Ferriby, Brough
8.45	Cottingham, Beverley, Driffield, Bridlington, Filey, Seamer, Scarborough
8.45	Goole, Doncaster, London (King's Cross) (restaurant car, Doncaster to King's Cross)
9.00	Brough, Selby, Leeds (City), Huddersfield, Manchester (Exchange), Liverpool (Lime Street) (restaurant car)
9.12	Brough, Goole, Thorne (North), Doncaster, Sheffield (Midland)
9.24	Brough, Goole, Stainforth & Hatfield, Doncaster, Sheffield (Victoria), Manchester (Central), Liverpool (Central) (buffet car)
9.25	Hornsea and intermediate stations (except Swine, Whitedale)
9.40	Withernsea and intermediate stations
9.45	York and intermediate stations (except Warthill, Earswick) (SO calls Fangfoss)
10.00	Goole and intermediate stations
10.00	Cottingham, Beverley
10.32	Goole, Doncaster, London (King's Cross) (THE YORKSHIRE PULLMAN, supplementary charges)
10.35	Scarborough and intermediate stations (except Burton Agnes, Speeton, Gristhorpe)
10.45	Selby, South Milford, Micklefield, Cross Gates, Leeds (City), Bradford (Forster Square)
10.50	Brough, Goole, Thorne (North), Doncaster
11.00	SO Goole and intermediate stations
11.40	SO Cottingham, Beverley

PM	
12.03	SO Brough, Staddlethorpe, North Howden, Selby and intermediate stations to Leeds (City) (except Osmondthorpe, Marsh Lane)
12.10	SO Withernsea and intermediate stations
12.12	Cottingham, Beverley, Market Weighton, Pocklington, Fangfoss, Stamford Bridge, Earswick, York
12.15	SO Stainforth & Hatfield and intermediate stations
12.20	Brough, Goole, Thorne (North), Doncaster, Retford, Newark, Grantham, Peterborough (North), London (King's Cross) (buffet car, Doncaster to King's Cross)
12.25	Hornsea and intermediate stations
12.30	SX Cottingham, Beverley
12.30	SO Cottingham, Beverley, Driffield, Bridlington
12.30	Selby and intermediate stations
12.40	Withernsea and intermediate stations
12.45	Hessle, Ferriby, Brough
12.45	SX Cottingham, Beverley, Driffield, Bridlington
12.45	SO Cottingham, Beverley, Driffield, Bridlington, Flamborough, Bempton, Filey, Scarborough
12.55	SO Botanic Gardens, Stepney, Wilmington, Sutton-on-Hull, Ellerby, Hornsea Bridge, Hornsea
1.00	SO Cottingham, Beverley
1.08	Selby, Leeds (City)
1.20	Bridlington and intermediate stations, Bempton, Filey, Seamer, Scarborough
1.25	SX Botanic Gardens, Stepney, Wilmington, Sutton-on-Hull, Ellerby, Sigglesthorne, Hornsea Bridge, Hornsea
1.30	SX Hessle, Ferriby, Brough
1.30	SO Thorne (North) and intermediate stations
1.40	Withernsea and intermediate stations
1.45	Cottingham, Beverley
1.55	SO Botanic Gardens, Stepney, Wilmington, Sutton-on-Hull, Ellerby, Sigglesthorne, Hornsea Bridge, Hornsea
2.02	Selby, Leeds (City), Huddersfield, Manchester (Exchange), Liverpool (Lime Street)
2.15	Hessle, Ferriby, Brough
2.20	SX (commences 26/5/58) Cottingham, Beverley, Driffield, Bridlington and intermediate stations to Scarborough (except Speeton)
2.25	SO (commences 17/5/58) Cottingham, Beverley, Driffield, Bridlington, Hunmanby, Filey, Seamer, Scarborough
2.30	SO Doncaster and intermediate stations (except Barnby Dun)
2.30	SX Goole and intermediate stations, Snaith
2.45	SX Goole, Thorne (North), Doncaster, Peterborough (North), London (King's Cross), also Sheffield (Victoria)
2.50	Leeds (City) and intermediate stations (except Broomfleet, Hambleton, Marsh Lane)
3.00	Cottingham, Beverley, Market Weighton, Pocklington, York
3.15	Cottingham, Beverley
3.40	Withernsea and intermediate stations
3.45	Cottingham, Beverley, Driffield, Bridlington and intermediate stations to Filey, Scarborough
3.56	York and intermediate stations
4.00	Selby, Leeds (City), Huddersfield, Manchester (Exchange), Liverpool (Lime Street) (restaurant car)

Time	Destination
4.13	Hessle, Ferriby, Brough, Goole, Thorne (North), Stainforth & Hatfield, Doncaster, Sheffield (Vic.), Manchester (Cen.), Liverpool (Cen.)(buffet)
4.25	Hornsea and intermediate stations
4.30	Bridlington and intermediate stations
4.30	Hessle, Ferriby, Brough
4.40	Withernsea and intermediate stations
4.45	SX Cottingham, Beverley
4.50	Thorne (North) and intermediate stations
5.00	Brough, North Howden, Selby, Hambleton, South Milford, Micklefield, Garforth, Cross Gates, Osmondthorpe, Leeds (City)
5.10	SX Beverley, Driffield, Bridlington, Filey, Scarborough
5.15	Goole, Thorne (North), Stainforth & Hatfield, Barnby Dun, Doncaster, Retford, Grantham, Peterborough (North), London (King's Cross)
5.15	Cottingham, Beverley, Market Weighton, Pocklington, Earswick, York
5.18	Leeds (City) and intermediate stations (except Hambleton, Osmondthorpe)
5.25	Wilmington, Sutton-on-Hull, Ellerby, Hornsea Bridge, Hornsea
5.30	SX Beverley, Driffield, Bridlington
5.35	Wilmington, Southcoates, Marfleet, Hedon, Ryehill & Burstwick, Ottringham, Withernsea
5.45	Scarborough and intermediate stations (except Gristhorpe); (SO calls Carnaby)
5.48	Hessle, Ferriby, Brough
5.53	SX Goole, Doncaster
5.55	Hornsea and intermediate stations (except Swine)
6.10	Withernsea and intermediate stations
6.15	SO Cottingham, Beverley
6.20	Goole and intermediate stations
6.25	Hornsea and intermediate stations
6.35	Brough, Goole, Wakefield (Kirkgate)
6.40	Withernsea and intermediate stations
6.45	Cottingham, Beverley, Driffield, Bridlington
7.00	Doncaster and intermediate stations
7.10	Brough, South Eastrington, North Howden, Wressle, Hemingbrough, Selby, South Milford, Cross Gates, Leeds (City)
7.35	York and intermediate stations (except Cherry Burton)
8.15	Bridlington and intermediate stations
8.25	Hornsea and intermediate stations
8.35	Selby, Pontefract, South Milford, Micklefield, Garforth, Cross Gates, Leeds (City)
8.40	Withernsea and intermediate stations
8.45	Hessle, Ferriby, Brough
9.00	Cottingham, Beverley
9.15	Brough, Goole, Thorne (North), Doncaster (SO calls at Stainforth & Hatfield)
9.35	Goole and intermediate stations
9.40	TSO Withernsea and intermediate stations; (commencing 5th May 1958, runs daily)
9.45	Bridlington and intermediate stations (except Carnaby)
9.55	WSO Hornsea and intermediate stations; (commencing 6th May 1958, runs daily)
10.45	SO Goole and intermediate stations
10.45	SX Cottingham, Beverley
11.00	SO Cottingham, Beverley
11.33	SO Cottingham, Beverley

Key: **SO** Saturday Only; **SX** Saturday Excepted; **TSO** Tuesday and Saturday Only; **WSO** Wednesday and Saturday Only.

A3 no.60053 SANSOVINO departs Hull with an E.C.S. to Leeds in 1961. *Peter Harrod.*

WEEKDAY ARRIVALS AT HULL PARAGON STATION (16th September 1957 to 8th June 1958)

AM	FROM
12.17	MO Leeds (City), Cross Gates, Garforth, Micklefield, South Milford, Selby, Hemingbrough, Brough, Hessle
1.33	MO Doncaster, Goole
2.33	MX Doncaster, Goole
4.25	Leeds (City), Selby, Brough
4.56	MO York, Selby
5.04	MX York, Selby
5.17	London (King's Cross), Doncaster, Goole
6.38	Beverley, Cottingham
6.50	Stainforth & Hatfield, Thorne (North), Goole, Saltmarshe, Brough, Ferriby, Hessle
7.08	Bridlington, Driffield, Beverley, Cottingham
7.20	Leeds (City) and intermediate stations (except Hambleton, Ferriby, Hessle)
7.30	Withernsea and intermediate stations
7.33	Doncaster and intermediate stations (except Staddlethorpe, Broomfleet)
7.45	Hornsea, Hornsea Bridge, Ellerby, Sutton-on-Hull
7.48	Leeds (City), Osmondthorpe, Cross Gates, Garforth, Selby, North Howden, Brough, Ferriby, Hessle
7.53	Beverley, Cottingham
8.12	Goole and intermediate stations
8.15	Bridlington and intermediate stations
8.29	Hornsea and intermediate stations
8.35	Withernsea and intermediate stations
8.42	Goole and intermediate stations
8.46	Bridlington, Driffield, Beverley, Cottingham
8.54	Withernsea and intermediate stations (except Patrington, Keyingham)
8.55	Leeds (City) and intermediate stations (except Hambleton)
8.57	Beverley, Cottingham
9.06	Hornsea, Hornsea Bridge, Sigglesthorne, Ellerby, Sutton-on-Hull
9.19	Scarborough and intermediate stations (except Carnaby, Arram)
9.25	Brough, Ferriby, Hessle
9.26	York and intermediate stations
9.33	Scarborough, Filey, Bridlington, Driffield
9.47	Leeds (City), Cross Gates, Garforth, Micklefield, South Milford, Selby, Brough
10.15	Scarborough and intermediate stations (except Gristhorpe, Speeton, Lockington)
10.20	Doncaster, Stainforth & Hatfield, Thorne (North), Goole, Staddlethorpe, Brough, Ferriby, Hessle
10.43	Beverley, Cottingham
10.53	Hornsea and intermediate stations (except Whitedale)
11.01	Leeds (City), Selby, North Howden, Brough
11.07	York, Pocklington, Market Weighton, Beverley, Cottingham
11.20	Withernsea and intermediate stations
11.43	Bridlington, Driffield, Beverley, Cottingham

PM	
12.13	SX Sheffield (Victoria), Doncaster, Barnby Dun, Stainforth & Hatfield, Thorne (North), Goole
12.23	SO Beverley, Cottingham
12.24	SO Sheffield (Victoria), Doncaster and intermediate stations (except Saltmarshe, Staddlethorpe)
12.32	SX Goole and intermediate stations
12.49	SO Goole and intermediate stations
1.03	Wakefield (Kirkgate), Goole
1.09	Leeds (City), South Milford, Selby, Brough (SO calls North Howden, South Eastrington)
1.13	Scarborough and intermediate stations (except Gristhorpe, Speeton, Carnaby)
1.41	Liverpool (Central), Manchester (Central), Sheffield (Victoria), Doncaster, Stainforth & Hatfield, Thorne (North), Goole, Brough
1.45	Brough, Ferriby, Hessle
1.46	York and intermediate stations
1.54	Hornsea and intermediate stations
1.54	SO Leeds (City), Cross Gates, Garforth, Micklefield, South Milford, Hambleton, Selby, North Howden, Brough
1.58	Beverley, Cottingham
2.04	SO Goole and intermediate stations
2.20	Withernsea and intermediate stations
2.24	SO Hornsea and intermediate stations
2.28	Beverley, Cottingham
2.30	SO Liverpool (Lime Street), Manchester (Exchange), Leeds (City), Selby, Brough
2.31	Brough, Ferriby, Hessle
2.38	SX Liverpool (Lime Street), Manchester (Exchange), Leeds (City), Selby, Brough
2.48	SX London (King's Cross), Doncaster, Goole, Brough
2.50	SX Hornsea, Hornsea Bridge, Sigglethorne, Ellerby, Sutton-on-Hull
2.52	SO Stainforth & Hatfield and intermediate stations
2.53	Scarborough and intermediate stations (except Burton Agnes)
3.01	SO London (King's Cross), Doncaster, Goole, Brough
3.17	Withernsea and intermediate stations (except Keyingham, Marfleet)
3.24	Brough, Ferriby, Hessle
3.24	SO Hornsea, Hornsea Bridge, Sigglesthorne, Ellerby, Sutton-on-Hull
3.48	Beverley, Cottingham
4.28	York, Stamford Bridge, Pocklington, Market Weighton, Beverley, Cottingham
4.41	Scarborough, Seamer, Filey, Hunmanby, Bempton, Bridlington, Burton Agnes, Lowthorpe, Nafferton, Driffield, Hutton Cranswick, Lockington, Arram, Beverley, Cottingham
4.44	SO Thorne (North) and intermediate stations
5.02	SX Snaith, Rawcliffe, Goole and intermediate stations
5.11	Sheffield (Midland), Doncaster, Barnby Dun, Stainforth & Hatfield, Thorne (North), Goole, Brough
5.15	Bradford (Forster Square), Leeds (City), Cross Gates, Micklefield, South Milford, Hambleton, Selby, Hemingbrough, Wressle, North Howden, South Eastrington, Staddlethorpe, Brough, Ferriby, Hessle

20

5.21	Withernsea and intermediate stations
5.24	SX Beverley, Cottingham
5.31	SX Bridlington and intermediate stations (except Lockington)
5.39	Brough, Ferriby, Hessle
5.51	Hornsea, Hornsea Bridge, Sigglesthorne, Ellerby, Sutton-on-Hull
5.58	SX Doncaster and intermediate stations (except Stainforth & Hatfield)
5.58	SX Beverley, Cottingham
6.20	York, Pocklington, Market Weighton, Beverley, Cottingham
6.25	Withernsea and intermediate stations
6.28	Sheffield (Victoria), Doncaster and intermediate stations (except Broomfleet)
6.29	Scarborough and intermediate stations (except Gristhorpe, Speeton)
6.34	Leeds (City), Selby, Wressle, North Howden, South Eastrington, Staddlethorpe, Brough
6.40	Hornsea, Hornsea Bridge
6.42	York and intermediate stations (except Kipling Cotes, Cherry Burton)
6.47	London (King's Cross), Doncaster, Goole, Brough
6.52	Brough, Ferriby, Hessle
7.08	SO Beverley, Cottingham
7.11	Withernsea and intermediate stations (except Keyingham, Marfleet)
7.22	Sheffield (Victoria), Doncaster, Barnby Dun, Stainforth & Hatfield, Thorne (North), Goole
7.24	Hornsea and intermediate stations
7.28	Bridlington and intermediate stations (except Lockington)
7.43	Withernsea and intermediate stations (except Patrington, Keyingham)
7.50	Hornsea, Hornsea Bridge, Ellerby
7.50	Liverpool (Lime Street), Manchester (Exchange), Huddersfield, Leeds (City), Selby, Brough, Ferriby, Hessle
7.57	Goole and intermediate stations
8.00	Scarborough, Seamer, Gristhorpe, Filey, Hunmanby, Bempton, Flamborough, Bridlington, Nafferton, Driffield, Beverley
8.17	Withernsea, Patrington, Ottringham, Ryehill & Burstwick, Hedon
8.21	York, Stamford Bridge, Pocklington, Market Weighton, Beverley, Cottingham
9.04	Bridlington, Driffield, Beverley, Cottingham
9.11	Liverpool (Central), Manchester (Central), Sheffield (Victoria), Doncaster, Stainforth & Hatfield, Thorne (North), Goole, Brough
9.32	London (King's Cross), Doncaster, Goole (THE YORKSHIRE PULLMAN)
9.46	Hornsea, Hornsea Bridge, Sigglesthorne, Ellerby
9.49	Goole and intermediate stations (except Broomfleet)
9.49	Beverley, Cottingham
10.07	SO Scarborough, Seamer, Filey, Hunmanby, Bempton, Flamborough, Bridlington, Driffield, Hutton Cranswick, Lockington, Arram, Beverley, Cottingham
10.17	Withernsea, Ottringham, Keyingham, Ryehill & Burstwick, Hedon
10.23	SX (commencing 26/5/58) Scarborough, Seamer, Filey and intermediate stations to Bridlington, Driffield, Hutton Cranswick, Lockington, Arram, Beverley, Cottingham
10.26	Brough, Ferriby, Hessle
10.36	London (King's Cross), Doncaster, Goole, Brough
10.43	York, Pocklington, Market Weighton, Beverley, Cottingham
10.44	Leeds (City), South Milford, Selby and intermediate stations
10.59	WSX Goole, Brough, Ferriby, Hessle
11.06	WSO Goole and intermediate stations (except Broomfleet)
11.14	London (King's Cross), Doncaster, Goole, Brough
11.20	TSO (commencing 5/5/58 runs daily) Withernsea and intermediate stations
11.23	SX Beverley, Cottingham
11.24	WSO (commencing 5/5/58 runs daily) Hornsea and intermediate stations
11.38	SO Beverley, Cottingham
11.58	SO Bridlington and intermediate stations (except Burton Agnes, Lockington, Arram)

Key: **MO** Monday Only; **MX** Monday Excepted; **SO** Saturday Only; **SX** Saturday Excepted; **TSO** Tuesday and Saturday Only; **WSO** Wednesday and Saturday Only.

D9 no.5112 arrives at Paragon with a stopping train from Sheffield (Victoria) at some time in the 1930's. This brought in the through coach from Swansea - the so-called 'Ports to Ports' express.
Authors collection.

NAMED ENGINES HAVING HULL CONNECTIONS

The London & North Eastern Railway gave the City's name to two engines, the first one being Raven Pacific 2401. It was the last engine built by the North Eastern Railway, being put into stock only on Dec.30th 1922, the day before the N.E.R. was merged as part of the LNER. Until April 1924, it did not have a name, but plates CITY OF KINGSTON UPON HULL were then fitted; needing a two-line plate, which was a distinct rarity. That engine was built to haul express passenger trains on the main line between Newcastle and Edinburgh, but by 1934 more puissant engines had superseded it, so 2401 was moved to York shed, from where it worked to and from King's Cross on trains such as the 'Norseman'. Between such workings, it occasionally came to Hull hauling the afternoon main line goods train from York via Beverley. At Cottingham South junction it took the direct line to Dairycoates yard over the level crossings at Waterworks (Spring Bank West), Newington (Anlaby Road), and Hessle Road. It then collected the outward Class E goods for York and the north, taking that via Brough, Selby, and Church Fenton. By going back to York that way it avoided having to be turned, and any further delays to road traffic at three of Hull's level crossings. Its overall length of 72' 7" overall, and 62' 2" wheelbase would have meant it being found a path round a triangle of lines, thus delaying traffic which normally used them, because Hull had no turntable greater than 60 feet diameter. Fortunately pictorial evidence of its visits can be provided, although taken between Hessle and Ferriby, so is outside the boundary with which this book deals.

From March to June 1936, the LNER works at Darlington built fourteen 4-6-0 engines of B17 class to which names of Association Football clubs in LNER territory were given. Below each club's name were painted panels of club colours, so that when 2860 began work on June 19th 1936 named HULL CITY, its panels were in ultramarine blue. At the start of the 1935-36 season the club had forsaken the traditional amber and black stripes, and had changed to that blue with white collar and cuffs. It proved a disastrous move, because of the 42 League matches they played that season, they won only five which relegated them from the Second to the Third Division (North). It did not take much 'spectator power' to get the blue also relegated, and from the start of the 1936 season they were back in the 'Tiger' stripes (but Hull City AFC did not go back up to the Second Division until the 1948-49 season). Engine 2860 however was shedded in Manchester, and normally worked the expresses to Sheffield, Leicester, and London (Marylebone); it is believed that it never worked into Hull. 2860 kept its blue panels until March 1942 when, as a wartime measure the engine was changed from green to unlined black, and the panels were also blacked over. In January 1947 the number was changed from 2860 to 1660, and in January 1949 British Railways made it 61660. The colour panels were not replaced until June 1951, and then amber and black stripes were duly applied. By then, all its work was being done in the Eastern Counties, which provided no opportunity for it to come to Hull. At the end of the 1959 summer timetable there was no work for it and as it was put into open storage at Lowestoft shed, the nameplates were taken off to prevent their being sto-

len, so it was nameless from 7th November. However in January 1960 it was transferred to March shed from which it worked regularly to Leicester until it was withdrawn (still nameless) on 2nd June 1960 to be scrapped at Stratford. British Railways then presented one of the pair of HULL CITY nameplates to the football club, who put it on display at Boothferry Park, mounted over the tunnel by which the players enter and leave the pitch, and where it can still be seen.

Those who just had a nodding acquaintance with passenger engines took scant notice of how they were numbered, and to such, 1010 and 1215 had little significance. But a mention of WILDEBEESTE, or WILLIAM HENTON CARVER would launch them into animated talk about either, or both, taking them by train to grammar schools they attended. Those two B1 class were shedded in Hull, WILDEBEESTE for the whole of its 19 years life, and WILLIAM HENTON CARVER from new in July 1947 until November 1962 when it was sent to work from Ardsley until its withdrawal in March 1965. Appropriately, it returned for Albert Draper to take to pieces, as he also did with WILDEBEESTE when it was withdrawn from service in November 1965.

(left) **Raven Pacific 2401 CITY OF KINGSTON UPON HULL heads back to York with a goods train from Hull.**
T.E.Roundthwaite.

(opposite top) **B17 no.2860 HULL CITY at its Gorton (Manchester) shed in 1937.**
W.L.Good.

(opposite bottom) **Inter City 125 power car no.43116 was named City of Kingston upon Hull on Monday 9th May 1983 at Paragon station. The ceremony was performed by the then Lord Mayor of Hull, Councillor H.Woodford. 43116 was in Paragon with the Sunday London train as recently as 26th February 1995.**
53A Models, Hull.

Even better known than the two named B1's were the 4-4-0's which did the bulk of Hull's passenger work from 1932 until the mid-1950's. They were the Shires, and the Hunts, known collectively as the D49's, and the number they got when new was changed in 1946 from a random to a consecutive series. So a mention of 238, or 2757, is likely to get a blank look, but say THE BURTON (the engine which carried those numbers) and you get immediate interest. Of the 76 in that class, at some time, 35 were shedded in Hull, and for ready recognition, here is a list of them. The 3-digit numbers are those they got from new, the 4-digit ones being those to which they changed in 1946, and to which British Railways added a 6 prefix from 1948.

HERTFORDSHIRE	256	2703
BANFFSHIRE	309	2717
CAMBRIDGESHIRE	318	2720
WARWICKSHIRE	320	2721
HUNTINGDONSHIRE	322	2722
NOTTINGHAMSHIRE	327	2723
BEDFORDSHIRE	335	2724
THE QUORN	336	2727
THE ALBRIGHTON	205	2751
THE YORK AND AINSTY	211	2737
THE ATHERSTONE	214	2752
THE ZETLAND	220	2738
THE BERKELEY	222	2754

THE HOLDERNESS	273	2744
THE CRAVEN	274	2759
THE COTSWOLD	279	2760
THE HURWORTH	282	2745
THE MIDDLETON	283	2746
THE SOUTHWOLD	292	2748
THE PYTCHLEY	298	2750
THE FITZWILLIAM	359	2763
THE GOATHLAND	362	2765
THE GRAFTON	363	2766
THE GROVE	364	2767
THE TYNEDALE	377	2775

YORKSHIRE	234	2700	THE BROCKLESBY	230	2756
LANCASHIRE	236	2707	THE BEDALE	235	2740
LINCOLNSHIRE	245	2710	THE BURTON	238	2757
DERBYSHIRE	251	2701	THE BLANKNEY	247	2741
OXFORDSHIRE	253	2702	THE CLEVELAND	269	2743

Three phases in the life of D49 'Hunt' THE ZETLAND *(below)* **as No.220 and in LNER green;** *(bottom left)* **as renumbered in 1946 and painted black, unlined;** *(bottom right)* **as BR No.62738 but in lined black.**

The 1906/7 rebuilding of SCULCOATES/WILMINGTON SWING BRIDGE

Bridge No.10 @ 2miles 19.98 chains.

The 3½ mile long Victoria Dock branch which was opened in 1853 had one necessary major engineering work, that required to take it across the River Hull, and the bridge design was complicated because it had to be capable of being opened, river traffic having precedence. The bridge's original name of Sculcoates stemmed from its location being in the parish of that name. From opening until 1st June 1864 that branch line had been single track, but it then needed to cope with the extra traffic resulting from the diversion of the Withernsea trains to Paragon station, and the opening of the Hornsea branch line, both of which had to use the bridge. So by that date, most of the Victoria Dock branch was converted to double track, except for the short section through Sculcoates station and across the swing bridge. Even there, it was worked as a double line, the additional line being 'interlaced' with the existing line, to save the cost of a new, and wider, bridge. By extending the interlacing as far west as Sculcoates Goods signalbox, the railway avoided spending money on building an extra platform at Sculcoates station. That track arrangement continued to be used

until 1912 and is clearly illustrated in one of the photographs on page 30. Then the opening of a new, and more conveniently situated, station on the opposite bank of the river at Wilmington Junction enabled the old Sculcoates single platform station to be closed.

When doing my research, I could find very little information about the structure of the bridge built in 1853, but it was wrought iron and about 108 feet overall length. Its erection was supervised by Thomas Cabry, who was the York & North Midland's engineer. It was strengthened more than once, but by the early 1900's its restrictions on both weight and speed could no longer be tolerated, replacement by a modern design being essential, and with normal arrangement for double track. The North Eastern Railway had already successfully surmounted a similar problem where the East Coast main line crossed the Ouse at Selby, so an almost identical design was chosen to cross the Hull at Wilmington, although with a slight, but very significant, difference. At the insistence of Hull Corporation, the Wilmington bridge had to include provision for a public footpath across it. That was provided by fixing suitable brackets to the outside of the north main girder to support a walkway 6 feet wide, meeting the Corporation's stipulation easily and at small cost. Then, in the 1960's the various rail services

using the bridge ceased to operate and, but for the right of foot passage, British Rail would undoubtedly have demolished the bridge, thereby saving themselves the cost of its maintenance, and that of manning it for the benefit of traffic on the river, in which they had not the slightest interest. They managed to pass that over to Hull Corporation, and the walkway now goes between the two main girders.

With the new bridge having to be constructed in close proximity to the existing one, inevitably there was disruption to the working of the 1853 bridge, which had to be minimised by the construction of a temporary foundation on the east bank of the river, at a point just clear of the old bridge when open for river traffic, and of the east abutment of the new one. Any other site, either north or south, would have involved sharp curves in the railway, and also increased costs by interference with nearby buildings.

For the new bridge the clear waterway was increased from the existing 37ft 6ins to 53ft 6ins, and under the east (the land) arm, for an additional waterway of 40 feet because of proposed widening of the river. That needed considerable dredging of the river bed, the setting back of the west abutment, and the provision of a substantial river wall about 100 yards long. The work involved can be readily appreciated from the photograph dated 25th October 1906.

So far this is the only picture to have come to hand showing both the original Wilmington bridge and a train, or more correctly a locomotive. Here we are viewing the bridge from the west bank of the River Hull, at some time during the early summer of 1906 with pile drivers doing preparatory work on the opposite bank. The locomotive, NER 901 Class 2-4-0 No.370 was built at Gateshead works in August 1881 and was withdrawn by the LNER in October 1924 from Darlington shed; a sister engine, No.910, is happily preserved in the National Collection. *Memory Lane, Hull.*

The old bridge 11th June 1906. This view, taken from virtually the same vantage point as the previous picture, shows further evidence of work being carried out on both banks in readiness for the new swing bridge. On the extreme left is one of the 150 foot lattice masts erected by McKenzie & Holland to carry the electricity supply for the new bridge. The river is in a state of low tide and at periods such as this barge traffic could easily negotiate this stretch without the bridge having to open. The industry on the north side of the bridge is all situated on the west bank. *Authors collection.*

Local conditions had considerable influence on the design of the new bridge. The level crossing immediately to the west dictated that the rail level over the new bridge could not be raised more than 12 inches, otherwise it would not be possible to retain the existing road crossing.

The new bridge was built on a skew of $75\frac{1}{2}$ degrees, with a span of 160 feet, and excluding the outside walkway, was 29 feet 6ins wide between the centres of the main girders. They had plate webs, were hog-backed, 14 feet deep at the centre, and 7 feet at each end. The bridge floor had rail bearers, with cross bearers 9 feet apart, and at its centre were two special cross girders which, through a forged steel crosshead and two steel suspension bolts, transmitted the whole weight of the bridge to the central pivot on which the bridge turned. Before installation, the steel crosshead, and the cast iron pivot, were both tested with a proof load of 500 tons, which was 50% more than the load to be carried.

Temporary foundations on the east bank of the river provided the construction site for the new bridge which, after completion, it was intended to balance in situ before hauling it into place, but settlement under the centre pier prevented that being done. Then, on the completion of construction, the bridge and its operating machinery, was moved into position along a path comprising of a double row of piles with way-beams bearing a double line of rails under each main girder. The bridge was carried on eight six-wheeled bogies, placed as close to the centre of the bridge as possible, four under each main girder, and all of them able to carry a load of 90 tons. So that the central pivot, projecting below the bridge, could clear the east abutment and also the top of the roller path on the central pier, when moving the bridge into position, erection and launching had to be at a level of 3ft 10ins above its permanent working height. A locomotive hauled the bridge into its working position, its pull being augmented about twelve times by a block and tackle arrangement through which the haulage cable was passed. The bridge moved freely, but there was delay when two of the rails on which it was travelling broke at the edge of the abutment, that breakage also causing a tyre to shear off a bogie under both main girders, but progress was soon resumed. When the bridge reached its position on the central pier, hydraulic jacks took over to lower it into place. Weight of iron and steelwork in the bridge was about 460 tons, and the launch weight was 500 tons.

The bridge swung on a steel roller path which had eight steadying rollers. If need arose to renew the bearing discs and take the weight off the centre pivot, enough rollers were included to enable the bridge to be turned as usual. To facilitate this, the four centre cross girders were designed to take the abnormal loads which that would induce. Under the bottom flanges of the main girders at each end of the bridge, wedges slid into rest plates at the corners of the two abutments, being provided to take out the droop of the bridge after swinging, and also to secure it in place for safe passage of rail traffic.

The central pier carrying the pivot and the roller path was constructed entirely of 6 to 1 concrete, as also were the two abutments, and their foundations went down to the clay which overlaid the chalk, the clay being about 22 feet thick. They were about 19 feet below Ordnance Datum and about 21 feet below low-water level. Due to the proximity of the old and new bridge, and to the nature of the ground being passed through, which was only silt and warp, there was great anxiety during the sinking of the foundations. Precautions were taken by means of trestles, strutting, and tying back of the centre pier and abutments of the existing bridge to prevent settlement or movement, as far as possible. Only a single walled coffer-dam could be used for the centre pier; it was made of 12" square tongued and grooved piles, but they stood up very well. With the level of the roller path at 12.55 feet, and the highest recorded flood level being 15.38 feet, it was necessary to surround the top of the centre pier with a cast iron shield

A view of the north face of the original bridge on the same day in 1906 showing that both banks of the river below the bridge are crowded with industry of all sorts. Prominent on the east bank is the premises of Earle's Cement, the distinctive kilns rising above the factory. Established in 1811, the cement industry here was to outlive the railway but production ceased in 1970. In the river can be seen timber stanchions or guides erected to stop the occasional barge or boat from straying from its midstream course. Today, apart from the river, almost nothing of this scene remains. *Authors collection.*

3ft 6ins high, and to caulk the coffer-dam very thoroughly to ensure it was water-tight, and able to keep out the spring tides.

The machinery for inserting, and for withdrawing the wedges, also for turning the bridge, was housed in an overhead cabin, where it was duplicated; there was interchangeable hand-gear also for turning the bridge, and for operating the wedges. Two electric motors normally drove the operating mechanism, Hull Corporation supplying the power for them. Younger readers may not be aware that, prior to electricity being nationalised, numerous private companies could supply it, and in Hull, the Corporation had its own generating station, located at Sculcoates, but now demolished. The power for the bridge was conveyed across the river by an overhead armoured cable supported by 150 feet high lattice steel masts, the end of the cable being passed down through the roof of the operating cabin. A similar arrangement can be seen today at the Goole swing bridge. The series wound motors were supplied by Siemens Bros. Ltd, and running at 240 r.p.m. each could develop 30 h.p. at 440 volts. Each had a double-pole switch, an automatic cut-out, and fuses, with control by grid-iron resistances.

For swinging the bridge, the motors could be worked together, but each by its own controller. The copper commutator could take up to an inch of wear before needing renewal, and the quality of the carbon brushes guaranteed no sparking occurred until 50% above the normal

30 h.p. was reached. The electrical control panel had meters showing volts and amps and also dealt with the lighting in the cabin. Mechanical gear for the rotation of the bridge was by a bevel wheel and pinion, and then a long vertical steel shaft down to the circular rack on top of the foundations. The power required was approximately as follows:-

Withdrawing wedges 17.7 h.p. starting - 13.25 h.p. finishing; Swinging the bridge 26.5 h.p. starting - 17.70 h.p. finishing; Inserting wedges 13.0 h.p. starting - 14.75 h.p. finishing;

To ascertain the average time cycle - which was two minutes - the bridge was opened and closed thirty times, during which 12$\frac{1}{2}$ units of electricity were used.

To ensure that, when necessary, the wedges could be withdrawn by hand, two hydraulic rams were provided to take the weight off the wedges at each end of the bridge. The rams could lift 50 tons, the activating pump for them being close to the bridge operating gear in the overhead control cabin. In there were also the levers for working, and locking, the bridge and the footpath wicket gates, and for releasing the mechanical signal connections which passed over the bridge.

Originally the bridge was staffed by three men, an apprentice-trained fitter, who was in overall charge, assisted by two steersmen, their duties divided into three shifts. Three signalboxes were involved in the

working of the bridge, Wilmington on the eastern side, and on the western side, Sculcoates Goods, also Sculcoates Station, which was only 37 yards to the west of the road level crossing, whose gates it worked. That box took the leading part in the releasing, and swinging of the bridge.

When the bridge was to be opened for river traffic, the bridgeman, by ringing a single stroke bell (actually a conventional signalbox 'block bell') notified the signalman in Sculcoates Station box who, providing no train had been accepted, kept his signal levers at normal, and then pulled over the bridge release lever. Using a special "Plunging" instrument, he then indicated to the bridgeman that he was free to proceed. The bridgeman then back-locked the releasing lever in Sculcoates Station box, and operated the levers which worked the latch-bolt of the bridge to dis-engage the signal rodding, withdrew the wedges, and was then able to turn the bridge. As an extra safeguard, a modified form of "Lock and Block" working was in force between the three signalboxes concerned, for which special instruments were supplied by W.R.Sykes & Co., a well established firm of signal and telegraph engineers.

Plunging instruments were used only in the Sculcoates Station box, those in the boxes on either side of the bridge being of the non-plunging type. They gave the usual state of the line, and had bells to signal the class

of train. Immediately the signalman at either Sculcoates Goods, or at Wilmington Junction replaced the starting signal to "Danger" for the line leading to the bridge, the lever for it became electrically locked in the normal position, and remained so until again released by the Sculcoates Station man plunging his instrument. The signals for the lines approaching the bridge at all three boxes were so electrically controlled by the bridge wedges that the signal arms would not clear unless the wedges were proved to be fully home, and should the wedges have moved, or been displaced whilst a signal was off, the arm would at once be put to danger. Telephone communication was available between the three boxes, and between the bridge cabin and Sculcoates Station signalbox. The security of this method of working a swing bridge had been established by more than ten years experience of working an almost identical system at Selby bridge.

(above) **The new bridge was erected on the east bank, north of the existing railway, in line with its final position so that it could be rolled in when all was ready. This 7th September 1906 photograph shows work proceeding on the main girders of the new bridge whilst the surveyor checks alignments. The construction probably went on virtually unnoticed by the majority of people at the time, the local shipyards making as much noise and building larger items than the bridge.** *Authors collection.*

(opposite top) **A superb birds-eye view looking north-east on 25th October 1906. Just seven weeks separate this and the previous view yet the bridge is virtually complete, the main girders joined by the deck which is being made ready for the running rails. Work is now taking place erecting the upright girders on which the control cabin will be mounted. Until recent times this area of the city was its industrial heartland, a fact brought home when one counts the chimneys across the skyline; no less than forty are in view here.** *Authors collection.*

(opposite) **Nearly six months on and the new bridge is ready for rolling into its final position . The date is 15th April 1907 and preparations are made to roll out the old bridge once the new bridge is in position; notice the temporary line of rails laid alongside the old bridge. Whilst the two bridges are side by side neither can open for any river traffic. Rail access during the construction period was via a siding laid in temporarily at Wilmington Junction on the Down side and to the west of the then level crossing. The western extremity of the siding was upgraded and eventually formed part of the railway between the new bridge and the existing formation. Close examination of the photograph reveals at least a dozen wagons complete with permanent way staff busily engaged on this work. The exact date the new siding was brought into use is not known but it was inspected by the Board of Trade on 18th October 1905.** *Authors collection.*

15 APR 1907

Looking head-on at the western end of the new bridge in mid April 1907. Below the completed structure is the concrete pier on which it was to pivot. The workmen give a scale to the work and the diminutive size of the old bridge can be compared with that of the magnificent new bridge. As mentioned in the text, the new bridge was built someway above its final working position to enable the central pivot to clear the abutment during the rolling-in operation. Cantilevered onto the north, left-hand, side of the bridge is the public walkway, a necessary addition stipulated by an Act of Parliament.

(below) 15th April 1907 again but now the rain has ceased. We are now on the east bank of the river looking over the original span of the 1853 bridge towards Wincolmlee level crossing gates. This view shows to advantage the "interlacing" of the Up and Down lines necessary to cross the narrow bridge also, the locking mechanism for the bridge can be seen on the extreme right. Beyond Wincolmlee gates is the solitary platform of Sculcoates station, the two lines of track still interlaced. The temporary signal box erected 1905 and called Sculcoates Station stands to the left of the station, adjacent to the public entrance. This box was a replacement of the original signal box which had stood on the down side of the line and was demolished to make way for the new bridge; the temporary box was to remain in use for some time after completion of the bridge works whilst a new signalbox was erected on the line of the old formation. In the far distance is the bowstring girder bridge carrying the H&BR main line to Cannon Street station.

Within hours of commissioning the new bridge, the old bridge was lifted from its bearings and rolled onto the solid ground of the east bank as this 7th May 1907 view shows. It soon becomes apparent that removing the 1853 span was a scaled down reversal of rolling in the new bridge. In the background and just behind the remaining fixed span can be seen the level crossing gates across Wincolmlee, these, as other pictures show, had been in place for some time, but were only brought into use with the opening of the new bridge. Above the gates is the Down Main Home signal (top) with Wilmington Junction Distant signal. The roof of Sculcoates Goods station is beyond.

Taken shortly after the previous view, the old bridge is now clear of the river and ready for dismantling. To lighten the load, the running rails and timber waybeams were removed. Next job was to dismantle the turntable and caisson so that the new bridge was able to swing open for river traffic. Notice on the approach to the new bridge that only the Down line was in place; so it seems probable that 'Single Line Working' was in force at this time.

Looking east from the fixed span of the old bridge we can appreciate the contractors working confines between the old and new structures. Earle's cement factory, whose raw materials and finished products crossed both bridges in vast tonnages over the years, dominates the skyline on the right. The lattice mast is the twin of that seen earlier and carried the electric current for the new bridge.

The first train on Wilmington new bridge believed to be Friday 3rd May 1907. Although reproduced at least once before, no apologies are offered for using this picture which according to the late Ken Hoole was taken on the 10th May. By reference to other views in this collection, and with certainty it was taken prior to Tuesday 7th May when the old bridge was rolled back. On the left of this view a steam crane is busy stripping the old bridge which is still in situ and, allowing for the weekend and the jacking up of the old bridge prior to its roll-back we could safely say this was 3rd May. We respectfully suggest when the late Ken Hoole quoted the first train to use the new bridge as 10th May 1907, he was referring to possible normal double line working.

This splendid vision of things past was captured on the 11th May 1907 and is probably the first opening for river traffic by the new bridge. The name of the vessel is HALYCON.

Wincolmlee level crossing, Thursday 20th July 1967. Only yards away from their destination, two Type 1 diesels double head the Hessle Quarry - Earles Wilmington cement works chalk train. The second engine is D9547 but the leading engine's number is unknown. A lady looks on and waits patiently for the train to pass hopefully not discharging any dust from its load. Although only 37 yards separated the signal box and the swing bridge they had completely different names - the former taking its name Wincolmlee from the street, and the bridge from the area - Wilmington. *The Rev.David Benson.*

Wincolmlee, looking west from the control cabin of Wilmington swing bridge 20th July 1967. In all probability this is the return empty working of the train in the previous picture. On the skyline can be seen the bridge carrying the former H&BR Cannon Street line which at this date was still in daily use. Notice the kink in the new formation created by slewing the line for the new bridge; the previous alignment was virtually straight. The signal box stands on what was the old formation and behind it is waste land where Sculcoates station, closed 9th June 1912, once stood. *The Rev. David Benson.*

During the summer of 1907, but some time after the opening of the replacement swing bridge, a new signal box, which had originally been called Sculcoates was brought into use. This, like its temporary predecessor was on the Up side of the line. These new works were inspected by the B.o.T. on 6th August 1907. The locking frame, which consisted of 46 levers and gate wheel, was a McK & H No.16 type. At the time of inspection only 12 levers were in use and the track layout remained very much that of the original Sculcoates station even down to the interlacing through the platform which continued until 1912. By late 1923 and with the addition of a new Up siding for Major's oil depot, the track layout had reached its final form. The new siding connection was inspected by the Ministry of Transport on 22nd October 1923 ... "New Up siding and trailing points to Up main via slip road in cross over, extra signal"... "existing frame 17 spare levers." Things remained much the same for almost 40 years until colour light signals were provided on the main lines about 1960. It also seems that at this time the frame was shortened, and the first 15 levers were removed. With the run-down of goods facilities, and apart from a solitary trailing trap point protecting the swing bridge, all pointwork and shunting signals were removed in 1965, and for the last 3 years of its life Wincolmlee had only 11 working levers but at least it had its name in Gill Sans lettering. *Nick Fleetwood.*

THE RAILWAY/ELECTRIC TRAMWAY CROSSINGS OF HULL

When the railways, and electric tramcars, were both at their zenith within the City of Hull there were six locations at which these two forms of railed transport crossed on the same level. All six were also at road crossings, and on the North Eastern Railway because the Hull & Barnsley lines throughout the city were carried on a high embankment, and bridged the roads that they crossed. At five of those six crossings, in addition to the normal gates, special tram signals and catch points in the tramway were provided as an extra safeguard. It is not known who insisted on the safety measures being installed, but from photographs, it seems to have been the railway because the signals were of a McKenzie & Holland pattern as normally used by the NER in this area. The tram signals were worked mechanically in the lower quadrant, with the vertical operating rod placed inside the hollow post, not only for public safety, but to defeat any mischievous intent. These signals were electrically lit which was quite an innovation for the time. The maker's catalogue shows the rod connected to an angle crank in the base of the signal, below road level, and from it by means of a conventional wire run, connection would be made to the lever in the signal box. The catch points in the tram rails were worked by rodding as on the railway.

Prior to the arrival of electric traction in 1899, three of these crossings had, from 1877, tramcars hauled by horses, apparently without the need for protective means to prevent potential collisions. Only one tram route was worked by steam power, that across the NER's Victoria Dock branch at Hedon Road and which was no longer used by passenger trains. The crossing of those rails was relatively brief, being only from 22nd May 1899 until 13th January 1901, when the steam trams ceased to run, pending their conversion to electric traction. It was then at this crossing that the railway insisted on provision being made in order "to protect its interests".

In addition to the six crossings mentioned, the trams also crossed, on the level, the dock lines and sidings at Monument Bridge where they connected Prince's and Queen's Docks. At that location there were neither signals, catch points, nor gates, the traditional 'man with a red flag' being responsible for ensuring the safe passage of the occasional steam engine with its few wagons. The closure of Queen's Dock in 1931 eliminated that crossing.

Anlaby Road was the first to be used by the new trams when that rebuilt route opened on 5th July 1899, and had a life of 43 years and 2 months, the trams ceasing to run on 5th September 1942 on their replacement by trolley

In 1905 and nine years after the registration of the town's first motor car (Hull did not become a city until 1897), the horse and cart still retained an almost total monopoly. Displaying "S" in recognition of its Spring Bank route, tramcar No.116 the last of a batch of fourteen, all built by Milnes during 1903, waits obediently in Princes Avenue. The city bound tram, brought to a stand by one of the special tramway signals, is a sure indication as are the two horse drawn carts also stood waiting, that the gates though unseen are shut. On the right is the one and only building that comprised Botanic Gardens station and, apart from the window shutters, looked very much as it did 70 or more years later when it was demolished. To the left of Princes Avenue is the lodge and original entrance to the cemetery. To use the correct and full legal title The Hull General Cemetery Co. had a history roughly parallel to that of the nearby railway. The company was established in 1846 and opened for business the following year, 1849 saw a serious outbreak of cholera and many if not all of the victims are buried there. Eventually 20 acres were covered, 5 of which in 1859 were given over to the Local Board of Health no doubt for paupers graves from the Work House. The last known burial was some time in the late 1960s, eventually the company was wound up, and the land is now the property of the Hull Corporation.

The junction of Spring Bank and Princes Avenue at some time in the 1930's. The tram car, fleet number 124, was one of a batch of thirteen home made vehicles built by the Corporation at their Liverpool Street works during 1913/4. Heading towards the city centre, operating the "S" service, 124 originally had open balconies but was rebuilt as depicted here during the 1920's. Going in the opposite direction is an AEC 662 Regent double decker bus, Corporation fleet No.80, registration RH 4768. This bus was supplied new in 1932 and carried a Brush body. Apart from the fine display of contemporary road vehicles and posters - the Londesborough picture house was showing Charles Laughton and Laurel & Hardy - this picture illustrates the intersection of the tram and railway lines. Although the tram rails are broken, the rail lines are merely grooved to accommodate the passage of the tramcars. *Crich Tramway Museum.*

buses. Despite it being the busiest crossings by both rail and road, the additional protection of tram signals and catch points was never provided there. The existing splay-cornered signal box was retained to work their protective signals and gates.

The special crossings were supplied like all the other points and crossings on the tramway system by Messrs. Askam Brothers & Wilson, of Sheffield, and were all made of crucible cast steel. At the time of opening the tramway timetable catered for about 310 trams in each direction. These being spread across a working day of over 18 hours; commencing with the first departure at 5.30 a.m. and finishing with the last at 11.36 p.m. The road/rail level crossing was for the time quite an innovation and achieved much acclaim in the technical press...

"The level crossing in Anlaby Road is an excellent example of special work of a very difficult kind, and it reflects great credit on the makers. Special patterns had to be made both for the railway and tramway rails. Owing to irregular construction these were difficult to cast, and great care had to be exercised on this account in order to obtain straight and level castings. Some of the pieces weigh 800 lbs. each and are bolted down on timber plates and concrete"...*The Railway World, vol VIII, 10th August 1899.*

The Holderness Road route was the next one to be converted to electric traction, effective from 10th April 1900. It crossed the Withernsea passenger, and the Victoria Dock goods lines at Southcoates Station, the signal box working it simply carrying the name of Southcoates. Like at Anlaby Road, the cabin was splay cornered, but differed in that its operating area was built of wood. It dated from about 1877 when block working was introduced on the line. To give the signalman a clearer view of road traffic, a large bay window was provided at the end nearest the crossing. It was also here that the 'Tram frame' was installed, and at 90 degrees to the two existing main frames. Old records show, at about this time, a 'Main Frame' and a 'Shunting Frame', these being of 34 and 40 levers respectively, of which a total of 16 were spare. These records make no mention of the 'Tram Frame', but it would be similar to those at other boxes which had one, and which were only of 4 levers, one for release, one for signals, and two point levers. Whilst the catch points were worked independently, both tram signals would work at the same time. With the tram frame being at right angles to the main frame, how they were crossed-locked has yet to be ascertained. Fortunately an NER plan dated January 1900 for Southcoates shows the tram signals to have been behind the catch points, which were placed 60 feet from the gates, making that position the reverse of where it was normally on railway installations. Holderness Road tram service ceased on 18th February 1940, after which the tram signals and associated equipment were soon removed. Even so, the fittings under the signal box were still to be seen until Southcoates signal box was abolished in December 1968.

The first station out of Paragon on the Victoria

Dock branch, which also carried the Hornsea, and Withernsea trains, was first known as Cemetery, from 1866 as Cemetery Gates, and from 1st November 1881 as Botanic Gardens, and its use by passenger trains continued until 19th October 1964 when those two coastal stations were closed. Botanic Gardens station was adjacent to where the road known as Spring Bank divided into Spring Bank West and Princes Avenue, immediately to the west of where the tramway crossed the railway on the level. It was 2nd June 1900 before trams used that crossing, and horse trams never did so. When the electric trams replaced the horse trams the route was extended along Princes Avenue, but at first the service had to be operated with a break at the crossing 'owing to the railway Co. not yet having provided the necessary catch points and signal apparatus'. Until 8th October 1900, tram passengers thus had to dismount and cross the railway lines on foot, re-joining a tram on the other side. A separate 4-lever 'Tram Frame' was installed at 90 degrees to the main frame, but Botanic Gardens signal box did not have a bay window put in. Probably the catch points, signals, and frame controlling them would be altered later, because on 9th October 1913 a new route along Spring Bank West and also Newland Avenue was opened, and at the same time, a connection between that one and the Princes Avenue line was put in, making a triangular junction just to the west of the railway crossing. Almost certainly, that link would have needed the installation of at least one additional signal and catch point. Tram services over Botanic Gardens crossing ceased on 2nd October 1937, and at the end of that month the LNER put a new 'made up No.16 App.' lever frame in that signal box, and no doubt removed the tram frame. A survey carried out by the Tramway Department in January 1924 over three typical working days showed the gates were closed to road traffic for 25.2% of the time, compared with 17% some nine years earlier. During the 1924 survey, out of 1092 tram crossings, 488 were delayed for three or more minutes.

Stepney was the next station, and block post, on the Victoria Dock branch, and its level crossing affected the traffic on Beverley Road, the main artery out of the city to the north and north-west. The horse trams had crossed the railway there since 1877, and when electric traction replaced them on 8th December 1900, tram signals with catch points were installed, 78 feet and 75 feet from the crossing. Even so for a short time after the route was worked in two halves as the new Tramway/Railway crossing was not installed until the following month. This work commenced on Sunday 20th January 1901 but was not completed until Monday 28th. Then for some unknown reason another four weeks was to elapse before the Corporation saw fit to work trams across the railway as from Monday

25th February 1901. At some as yet unknown date a replacement signal box had been provided and it was from this that the new tram crossing was worked. A new frame with two gatewheels, installed on 10th February, were connected to the new and enlarged gates on the 14th February and as at Southcoates, Stepney signal box was given a bay window. When the Board of Trade Inspector made a further check of other new work on 23rd May 1903, his report contained no reference to the tram points or signals, but he included the double track tramway on his signalling plan, and both tram signals appear on a contemporary photograph. Stepney signal box was in use until 1968 when that part of the railway was closed, but the trams had ceased to run thirty years earlier because on 3rd September 1938, they had been superseded by trolley buses. The gates were mechanically worked to the finish, although about 1960, as an aid to both the signalman and road users, alternately flashing warning lights were installed, a very early example of those now associated with lifting barriers at road crossings. On 17th December 1903 a further tram route was converted to electric power, when the previously abandoned Hedon Road route was re-instated. When the Parliamentary Bill for the conversion had been read in the House of Lords on 29th June 1900, the NER opposed it on the grounds of public safety resulting in their Lordships now refusing to permit a double track electric tramway to cross the railway on the level. Whilst that was a set-back, it did have a beneficial result of Hull losing another of its irritating level crossings. There was political wrangling, because under an Act of 1886 the NER possessed extensive powers to regulate tram traffic at Hedon Road crossing. The North Eastern now objected totally to electric trams, and invoked Section 25 of the 1893 Hull Docks Act, in which if the Corporation desired to abolish the Hedon Road crossing, the NER were to construct a bridge over their railway lines, with the Corporation having to bear one-third of the cost. The railway company said that this was what should be done, and despite all their previous opposition to level crossings, on this occasion the Corporation clearly did not want a bridge. They claimed it would need approach roads with a gradient of 1 in 40, which would block side roads, and force heavy carts to need extra horses. But they were prepared to contribute to the cost of a railway bridge over the road. Naturally the NER strongly contested that demand, but were prepared to give it consideration. So a compromise agreeable to both parties was reached by which the railway company would build a bridge near to the site of the crossing, and raise their line by another 7$\frac{1}{2}$ feet because it was already 3$\frac{1}{2}$ feet above the general level of the road. For its part, the Corporation had to lower the level of the road, and

also compensate the railway for the land that they had to take to widen the road. One third of the cost was met by Hull Corporation, the NER paying the balance. It proved only a fine weather solution for the road users, because it put the resultant road below the normal sea level, and flooding closed it after any excessive rainfall, and also when high tides in the rivers Hull and Humber caused drains to back up.

Eleven years then passed before the next problem of a tramway crossing railway lines occurred. That resulted from the extension of the Hessle Road route at the level crossing and signal box of the same name in the area known as Dairycoates. Although the westward extension was brought into use on 16th February 1914, regular crossing of the trams did not start until 2nd June 1915, the route having to be worked in two halves. The cause of that delay was a shortage of labour due to the outbreak of the 1914 war. Here whatever the previous arguments, it was quite impossible to do other than retain the existing level crossing due to the position of the two bridges carrying the H&BR goods lines to Neptune Street over the NER and also over Hessle Road. No details of a separate tram frame are known, and maybe such a frame was never installed there, spare levers in Hessle Road signal box being adapted for that purpose, but a squared-off window was put in. That served two purposes - it helped the signalmen to see approaching trams but it also afforded a good view under the H&BR bridge. An unusual feature of that signal box was its flat roof at the end nearest the level crossing to accommodate the foot bridge of standard height, but caused the windows of the signal box to be reduced in height. When erected, in the early years of the war, the footbridge cost £550, the Corporation paying half, and at the same time, they paid the NER for 32 square yards of land needed for road widening. Hessle Road, with its 107 levers and 2 gate wheels, was the largest signal box in the city to work a level crossing.

After the railways were Grouped on 1st January 1923, the London & North Eastern Railway was more than two years old before the next, and what proved to be Hull's final tram crossing of tram and railway was brought into use. On Monday 5th October 1925 the Anlaby Road service was extended westwards to a terminus at Pickering Road which added two crossings to that route, making it the only tram route within the city to cross two railways. The first was at Newington, on the line which in 1845 had been built by the York & North Midland (George Hudson's own) Railway to link Hull with Bridlington. That section of it was only used for passenger trains until Paragon station was opened in May 1848, but the single line at Newington had been made double track in 1899 and was quite heavily used both for

This circa 1960s view is looking more or less towards the east and is taken from the foot-bridge once to be found on the west side of Botanic Gardens level crossing. The unidentified trolleybus operating on route 62 is about to leave Spring Bank and turn right to join Princes Avenue. Unlike the trams they replaced, trolleys did not have controlling signals at approaches to crossings. Regretfully this is yet another undated view, and apart from illustrating how the railway, after more than 100 years of continuous existence blended in so well with its surroundings, it also shows to advantage the normally unseen bits on the trolleybuses roof. In the Down platform of Botanic station is a four car d.m.u. bound for either Hornsea or Withernsea, and looking on are two young schoolboys both pupils at the nearby Hymers College. The leafless trees and heavy overcoats indicate a winter scene.
Mick Davies Collection.

goods trains, and for excursion trains originating inland and bound for the coast and so did not need to call in Hull. When the line was doubled, platforms were also put in at Newington to serve a showground near to it, and a new timber built signal box of the current 'S1' type was erected at the crossing, having a gate wheel and 12 levers, one of which was spare. That station went out of use in 1906, and before Grouping, the signal box had been reduced to just a 'gate box'. However, to facilitate trams crossing, on 8th June 1925 the LNER placed an order with the Westinghouse Brake & Saxby Signal Co. for frame No.9584 which was of 14 levers, and would cater for operating the tram signals and catch points. Newington had the shortest life of Hull's tram/railway level crossings because, from 29th July 1934 the tram route was cut back to its original length. Even so, trams continued to cross, the Tramway Department, for operational purposes, having retained a run-round loop to the west of the crossing, on the understanding that only empty trams would cross the railway lines. When Anlaby Road trams were superseded by trolley buses on 6th September 1942 that arrangement ceased. Both the gate box and level crossing continued to be used until 23rd May 1965 when that part of the 1845 line was able to be closed, a diversionary route becoming available through a curve being put in between West Parade North and South Junctions.

Two more of these tram/railway crossings might well have been added, both on the same route, and no more than a mile apart. On 9th October 1913 the Spring Bank route was extended westwards to terminate only a few yards short of the gates at Walton Street level crossing. After the 1914-18 war there was considerable development of new roads and housing on the country side of that crossing, making a logical case

for extension of tram services to them. In July 1923 the Corporation resolved to seek Parliamentary powers to do so, the intention being to extend the line along the full length of Spring Bank West and then along Calvert Lane to a junction with the Anlaby Road route. It would have been very interesting to see how they proposed to obtain the height for clearance under the H&BR's three bridges over Calvert Lane. In the proposed Bill was also a tram service along Hawthorn Avenue to link the Anlaby Road and Hessle Road lines, which would have needed yet another crossing of railway lines by the trams. Although the Spring Bank West extension part of the Corporation's 1923/24 Parliamentary Bill was approved, the Hawthorne Avenue section was rejected and also by that time the buses were casting their shadows over the trams.

In July 1924 the LNER laid a new line of rail from a junction on the former H&BR at Spring Bank North to Walton Street, which enabled them to divert passenger traffic into Paragon, and to close Cannon Street station. Signalling alterations were needed at Walton Street signal box and when making them the LNER prudently provided for any tramway crossing facilities they might have had to install should the Corporation get powers for extending the tramway. The replacement signal box at Walton Street included a frame of 27 levers and 2 gate wheels, because as the old box had done, the main, and wicket gates were worked by separate wheels. Some 7 levers, or almost 25% of this frame were spare, and it seems very credible that some of these were earmarked for future tramway use. It transpired that they were never needed, but in 1934 Walton Street became the first one in Britain to have conventional road traffic lights applied at a railway level crossing.

To the west of Walton Street was Waterworks

crossing where Spring Bank West crossed the 1845 Hull to Bridlington railway, and when that portion of it was doubled in 1899, a siding was also put in at Waterworks, but the existing box was retained to work the altered arrangement with its 9 levers. Arising from the rapid growth of housing development to the west of Hull, on 24th October 1924 the LNER placed an order with the Westinghouse Co. for the provision of gates and signals at that crossing costing £1021 18 shillings and 9d to be met in full by Hull Corporation. Surviving records then present different versions, one stating a frame of 20 levers was involved, the other indicating that only 7 levers and 2 gate wheels were those concerned. Certainly, the new box, of brick construction and 'Type S4' was big enough to take a 20-lever frame. Maybe the railway's original intention was to work any tram signals from the main frame as at Walton Street, but the failure of the Corporation's Bill was possibly known in time to avoid the expense of the larger frame, more than half of which would never have been used. Waterworks like Newington, was originally a block post, but was reduced in status to a gate box during 1932, and then remained so until the line was closed on 23rd May 1965.

A curious additional item worth a mention is that at one time the Corporation Tramway Department operated a signal box of its own. Situated on the Anlaby Road forecourt of Paragon station, it was used to regulate the trams at the junction of Midland Street and Anlaby Road and the signals were the same type as those used at the tram/railway crossings.

Although this picture is undated I suspect it was taken on a summer Sunday, probably during 1962/3. Several factors suggest this, the train, a d.m.u. is already well laden with passengers, and most likely consists of six or more cars. The policeman's "Dustbin" in which he would stand when directing traffic is conspicuous by its absence. Also leaning against the fence the local newsagent has left his billboard advertising his newspapers. The trolleybus, fleet number 116, registration RKH 116, was one of the "Coronation Class" a design unique to the Hull Corporation Transport Department. As one might suspect these vehicles originated from 1953, but were not actually purchased until 1954/55, and all survived until 1964 the final year of trolleybus operation in the city. The class of 14 vehicles were the last trolleybuses to be bought by the Corporation, and 116 was the very last one. Coincidentally both forms of transport came to an end within a fortnight of each other, the Hornsea and Withernsea passenger trains on Saturday 17th October 1964, and the trollybuses on Saturday 31st. *the late Robert Mack.*

Botanic Gardens 1958. Within seven years both the Princes Avenue trolley and the Hornsea and Withernsea passenger trains will be history. This picture if nothing else highlights the effects the city's level-crossings had on public transport. The 62 trolleybus services were timed to a 5 minute headway, but as the close proximity of these two illustrates, the passage of even one train would play havoc with the timetable. Eleven level-crossings lay across the various routes of the Hull Corporation Transport Dept, the majority were those operating to the west of the city, and apart from Beverley and Hessle Road with only one apiece most buses would pass over at least two crossings on their routes. Even worse off, were the Willerby and Wold Road routes which both encountered three railway crossings. Slightly better was east Hull with only the Holderness Road crossing as a major source of delay, but of course the gates at both Dansom Lane and Stoneferry all played their part from time to time. The signalman has opened the main gates, but the wicket gates remain firmly closed, this is intentional because in the past it had not been unknown for the opening wicket to catch up on the rear buffers of a departing train and be taken away with it. *the late Robert Mack.*

FORTY YEARS OF 4-6-2 LOCOMOTIVES VISITING HULL

The first of the LNER Pacifics to come to Hull was the special visit of 2569 GLADIATEUR for inclusion in the rolling stock exhibition held on 25th March 1928, which was mentioned in our previous book, and also illustrated. It did not work any passenger train either on arrival or departure.

The next Pacific to visit Hull was again for a rolling stock exhibition, in connection with the 1933 Civic Week, when the main railway display was in Paragon station on Sunday 15th October 1933. It was no less than 4472 FLYING SCOTSMAN, which had already established a reputation for reliably running the world-record non-stop 392 mile trains between King's Cross and Edinburgh. It must have been a deliberate choice because it was then shedded in London, and its visit did not coincide with being at Doncaster works for any repairs. Maybe the selection was influenced by one of the main visitors to the exhibition being the Lord Mayor of London, and at a lesser level, your author. Again, that engine came, and went, without working any passenger train. It was accompanied by an even bigger engine, the 4-6-2-2 high-pressure "hush-hush" No.10000, then allocated

to Gateshead shed, which also made solo journeys for the event. For a week, from 30th May to 6th June 1935, we had that engine coming here daily from Leeds on a series of dynamometer car tests after it had been fitted with a double blast-pipe and chimney, and using the counter-pressure engine No.761 to provide the loading. For the return journey they had to turn on the triangle of lines at Dairycoates because 10000 was much too long for our 60 foot turntables. The Selby-Hull line was chosen for the tests because it had an 18 mile stretch of straight line, also practically level, which eliminated variables due to gravity, curvature, and changing wind direction. On one test, nine miles were run at a constant 61 miles per hour, followed by eight miles at 60 m.p.h. producing horse-powers in the region of 1500, under conditions not open to any query.

Pre-war, the only Pacific which came to Hull on a revenue earning service was No.2401 CITY OF KINGSTON UPON HULL, which on a number of occasions between February 1934 and January 1936, brought the afternoon goods from York via Beverley, and returned with the outward goods via Selby and Church Fenton,

which avoided any need for turning at Dairycoates.

The next known sighting of a Pacific in Hull, and also on a goods train from York, was by a percipient, but absolutely reliable teenager, and was such as to almost cause him disbelief at what he was seeing. Whilst on his way to Kingston High School, his bus was (as usual) held up at the Dairycoates level crossing, but what was to be a day different from all others because, from the front seat of the bus, he saw it was painted black 4472 with just N E on the tender that was in charge. Probably it was being 'run-in' by Doncaster shed after the general repair from which it was ex-works early in April 1943.

More than another ten years were to pass ere we had a Pacific here on a normal passenger working; that was from and back to Leeds, although the engine was on York shed's allocation. It was 60515 SUN STREAM, of class A2/3, one of Edward Thompson's designs, and the local newspaper must have been told about the event, because on Wednesday 7th April their photographer turned out to take its picture as it was about to leave Paragon on the 9.02 a.m.

Thompson A2/3 no.60515 SUN STREAM waits for the departure whistle with the 2 minutes past nine morning train to Liverpool. This Wednesday 7th April 1954 view is the only known photographic record of an A2 working into Hull. *Hull Daily Mail.*

The 1969 visit by preserved A4 no.60019 BITTERN remains something of a mystery. *Hull Daily Mail.*

train to Liverpool (Lime Street) which it would only take as far as Leeds. That Pacific working does not seem to have lasted more than a week and none, other than 60515, was either seen, or reported, by the youthful enthusiasts of that period.

After about another four years bringing us to 1958, Leeds (Neville Hill) shed treated us to regular Gresley Pacific working from their own allocation. Nos. 60081, 60086 and 60088 named respectively SHOTOVER, GAINSBOROUGH and BOOK LAW (all winners of the Derby and/ or St Leger) came here frequently on the through trains from, and to Liverpool (Lime Street), but in 1961 these trains were turned over to the Trans-Pennine diesel railcar sets. Peppercorn Pacific 60140 BALMORAL although shedded at York, was seen working out of Paragon, and with the same Class H lamp code, rather more curiously, Gateshead based 60053 WOOLWINDER was photographed outward bound speeding alongside Selby Street sometime in 1961 (see page 19). In February 1964, 60156 GREAT CENTRAL was seen at Dairycoates, having worked in from its York shed on an afternoon goods.

On Monday 12th August 1957 we had the only known occasion of a Gresley streamlined A4 working out of Hull, 60005 SIR CHARLES NEWTON, piloted by BR Standard 2-6-0 No.77010, was on the 2.50 p.m. all stations train to Leeds. As there were two well loaded fish vans immediately behind 60005's tender, it would have every incentive to get a move on, to get out of the way of the smell especially if that August afternoon was a warm one.

British Railways ceased to use steam locomotives in 1968, but the following year we were regaled with two more Pacific appearances, both engines privately owned and in running condition. One made only a fleeting visit in the summer, coming from its then home at York. It was 60019 BITTERN and our local newspaper was once again on hand to record it photographically as it backed out of Paragon station. The purpose of the visit does not seem to have been revealed.

However, there was to be one Pacific momentous working for us to enjoy. To celebrate their 21st anniversary, the Hull Miniature Railway Society organised a day return outing to Edinburgh on Sunday June 8th 1969, and invited those who were interested to share it with them. 4472 FLYING SCOTSMAN was engaged to

leave Hull at 8.30 a.m., run the round-trip of 522 miles, allow us just over four hours free time in Edinburgh, and have us back at Hull in an overall time of 16 hours. For a 46-year old engine it was no mean feat to run the 261 miles in 5 hours and 45 minutes (including stops in York and Newcastle for crew changing), and to then repeat it only 4 hours and 15 minutes later. So FLYING SCOTSMAN made an equally distinguished visit to Hull as it had done when on ceremonial parade 36 years earlier.

There were two visits to Hull by 4-6-2's which were complete strangers, and which owed nothing to LNER influence. On 18th March 1967 Britannia class 70025 WESTERN STAR brought a train of football supporters from Barrow in Furness. Although outside our area, it is of interest to mention that its return journey had to be via Goole because Selby bridge was out of action due to a barge having stuck in the mud beneath it.

Preserved SR 'West Country' Pacific 34092 CITY OF WELLS came on 16th March 1988 simply to be filmed in Paragon station for a television commercial. I mention it to record my awareness, but prefer to say "no comment".

4472 FLYING SCOTSMAN departs from Paragon on the Hull Miniature Railway Society special to Edinburgh in June 1969. *Authors collection.*

Unlike their LNER counterparts, which from the mid 1950s were seen from time to time in the city, the BR Standard Pacifics were practically unknown. We are aware of three visits by these engines to Hull, and of these, the only one known by your author to have been recorded on film, was Britannia 70025 WESTERN STAR seen here about to pass under the Anlaby Road flyover whilst working train 1X33, a Barrow Rugby League supporters special back to the west coast on Saturday 18th March 1967. Almost certainly this would be the last time a member of this class, or for that matter, apart from preservation, a Pacific locomotive of any description worked into the City. 70025 first entered traffic in September 1952 allocated to the Western Region and working from Cardiff Canton shed. After a tragically short and totally uneconomic life of just over 15 years 70025 was withdrawn from Carlisle Kingmoor shed in December 1967. *The Rev.David Benson.*

MOTIVE POWER BASED IN HULL 1923 TO 1987

Rail 'ways' were laid to make movement of people and commodities easier, quicker, and smoother, but they were only a facility for doing so; some form of locomotion had to be provided. For the first public opening of a 'railway' in Hull, which took place on July 2nd 1840, a steam locomotive (popularly termed an engine) running on six wheels was responsible. The steam engine's basic principle of operation remained substantially un-changed through to the end of its use, at Hull in 1967, although size and power increased dramatically, those needing 12 wheels ultimately being used in this area. But the steam locomotive was labour intensive to a very high degree, and it is difficult now to realise that, just in Hull, it provided jobs (for both sexes) totalling some thousands. The days when almost every boy's ambition was to be an 'engine driver' are long gone, and for more than a century, the smoke, coal-dust, sparks and ashes inevitable with steam engines were accepted as just part of the job. The Clean Air Act hastened their end, and they had no friends in the environmental lobby. At least with smoke you could take avoiding action because you could see it, so it is ironic that their place has been taken by the internal combustion engine, from which pour noxious fumes of toxic gases largely unseen, and the hitherto blind eye to

their insidious nature has only recently been slightly opened. Maybe the medical cost of using diesel engines will soon be recognised as greater than the cost of electrifying what is then left of our railways.

But enough of moralising for the future because this is a 'history' and to know where we are going, we need to know where we have been. So a starting date of 1st January 1923 has been chosen, for three reasons (1) the LNER became effective that day, (2) precise documentation from then is available, and (3) the author was already a well-travelled railway enthusiast, even if not then in the Hull area: that began in earnest in 1931.

In an earlier joint work, (An Illustrated History of Hull's Railways *Irwell Press 1993*), brief reference was made to the various 'sheds' (known later as Motive Power Depots) at which engines were housed in Hull. They varied from one shed which was the home for only a single engine, to a shed with a complex of eight buildings responsible for looking after 146 locomotives at 1st January 1923. Of those, No.1076 built in March 1881 at a cost of £2149 was the oldest, the youngest then being No.905 new in November 1919 at a cost of £7609. The number of locomotives at that shed later grew to as many as 175 at the end of 1927.

When preparing the previous joint account, we had not located Hull's first engine shed, but have now found it shown on the 1853 Ordnance Survey map. It had three roads and the building was about 105 feet long and 25 feet wide with its south wall along Wellington Street. It was home to the eight 2-2-2 and two 0-6-0 which the Hull & Selby Railway owned, and after they were absorbed by George Hudson's York & North Midland Railway in 1846, also to any engines that bigger line sent to work the rapidly growing traffic. After the final transfer of the passenger traffic to Paragon station in 1854, what was known as Manor House station (although its frontage was on Railway Street) then only dealt with goods traffic, so the shed would retain some engines until Dairycoates opened in 1863, and by 1866 it had been merged into what became Hull's main goods station. The site of the Hull & Selby shed is now the boat yard for a thriving marina.

Traffic at Hull's first passenger station quickly outgrew what it was capable of handling, particularly with the opening of the line from it to Bridlington in 1845. By then, the public were appreciating the new facilities of rail travel, and the York & North Midland decided that there was need for a more central, and also a more impressive station for Hull.

Seven Class J77 0-6-0 tanks were transferred to Alexandra Dock in 1937 replacing engines condemned. No.948, photographed alongside the coaling stage in September 1938, was the oldest of them with origins going back to April 1874 when it was built by Neilson & Co. for the NER as a Bogie Tank Passenger with an 0-4-4 wheel arrangement. Rebuilt to NER 0-6-0 Class 290 at York in 1902, it survived to September 1948 as 8390 when it was withdrawn, still from the Alexandra Dock allocation. *Authors collection.*

Class	Number of engine when first allocated to Hull	Total

L.N.E.R. and B.R. types

Class	Number of engine when first allocated to Hull	Total
A5	9802, 9811, 9832, 9835, 9836, 9837	6
A6	686, 688, 690, 691, 694, 9791, 9793, 9796	8
A7	1113, 1114, 1126, 1129, 1136, 1170, 1174, 1175, 1176, 1179, 1180, 1182, 1183, 1185, 1190, 1191, 1193, 1195, 9781, 9787	20
A8	2147, 2148, 2151, 2153, 2159, 2160, 2161, 1517, 1520, 1521, 9859, 9876, 9877, 9878, 9879, 9880, 9881, 9882, 9886, 9888, 9894	21
B1	1002, 1010, 1012, 1032, 1060, 1065, 1068, 1071, 1074, 1080, 1084, 1094, 1176, 1215, 1255, 1256, 1289, 61303, 61304, 61305, 61306, 61322	22
B13	2001, 2003, 2004, 2009, 2010, 726, 738, 740, 744, 746, 747, 748, 749, 751, 752, 753, 754, 755, 756, 757, 758, 759, 760, 763, 768	25
B14	2111, 2112, 2113, 2114, 2115	5
B15	782, 786, 787, 788, 795, 796, 798, 813, 815, 817, 819, 820, 821, 822, 823, 824, 825	17
B16	840, 841, 842, 843, 846, 848, 849, 906, 909, 922, 925, 928, 930, 933, 934, 936, 937, 942, 943, 2365, 2367, 2369, 2377, 2379, 2380, 1371, 1373, 1374, 1375, 1376, 1378, 1382, 1384, 1385, 1404, 1416, 1419, 1420, 1426, 1435, 1437, 1441, 1443, 1444, 1452, 1453, 1460, 1462, 1463, 1466	50
C6	649, 295, 742, 1753, 1776, 1794, 696, 697, 698, 699, 701, 702, 703, 705	14
C7	709, 710, 718, 720, 722, 733, 736, 2165, 2167, 2168, 2169, 2170, 2172, 2195, 2196, 2198, 2199, 2201, 2203, 2204, 2206, 2207, 2208, 2209, 2211, 2212, 2970, 2982, 2995	29
C12	4019, 4514, 4517, 4519, 4520, 4524, 4534, 4541, 4542, 4543, 4544, 4545, 4546, 4547, 4549, 4550, 7350, 7352, 7353, 7354, 7361, 7382, 7389	23
D2	4180, 4386, 4387, 4398	4
D3	4074, 4075, 4077, 4080, 4301, 4304, 4313, 4341, 4345, 4346, 4347, 4348, 4349, 4350, 4354	15
D16/3	8817	1
D17/1	1620, 1622, 1623, 1626, 1628, 1629, 1630, 1632, 1633, 1634, 1635, 1638, 1639	13
D17/2	1871, 1873, 1874, 1905, 1907, 1909, 1910, 1922	8
D19	1619	1
D20	2013, 2014, 2016, 2017, 2018, 2024, 2026, 2101, 2102, 2103, 2108, 2109, 2110, 712, 1026, 1051, 1234, 1665, 2359, 2365, 2372, 2379, 2381, 2383, 2387	25
D21	1239, 1240, 1245, 1246	4
D22	42, 85, 96, 115, 117, 194, 230, 340, 356, 514, 663, 777, 803, 808, 1137, 1532, 1534, 1536, 1538, 1539, 1540, 1643, 1546	23
D23	23, 214, 222, 223, 258, 337, 521, 557, 675, 676, 677, 679, 1107, 1120	14
D24	2425, 2426, 2427, 2428, 2429	5
D49	234, 236, 245, 251, 253, 256, 318, 320, 322, 327, 335, 336, 2717, 205, 211, 214, 220, 222, 230, 238, 247, 269, 273, 282, 283, 292, 364, 377, 2740, 2750, 2759, 2760, 2763, 2765, 2766	35
E5	1468	1
F4	7175, 7184, 7578	3
F8	187, 262, 1322, 1582	4
G5	387, 435, 436, 441, 1334, 1691, 1693, 1701, 1703, 1737, 1740, 1755, 1882, 1884, 1888, 2082, 2084, 2088, 2091, 2092, 2098, 7253, 7254, 7261, 7263, 7266, 7274, 7284, 7312, 7337, 7241	31
G6	60, 247, 341, 358, 466, 605, 1055	7
J21	86, 97, 102, 122, 123, 139, 291, 294, 312, 316, 331, 431, 564, 568, 613, 665, 680, 778, 810, 874, 875, 876, 963, 973, 976, 981, 993, 1305, 1510, 1511, 1513, 1516, 1548, 1552, 1554, 1556, 1558, 1568, 1570, 1572, 1589, 1590, 1591, 1595, 1612, 1805, 1810, 1815, 5027, 5029, 5030, 5037, 5056, 5086, 5112	55
J22	422, 571	2
J23	2430, 2433, 2435, 2441, 2442, 2443, 2444, 2445, 2446, 2447, 2452, 2453, 2454, 2455, 2456, 2457, 2458, 2459, 2460, 2461, 2462, 2464, 2465, 2469, 2470, 2471, 2472, 2473, 2474, 2475, 2476, 2477, 2513, 2514, 2515, 2516, 2517, 2518, 2519, 2520, 2521, 2522	42
J24	1860, 1891, 1892, 1931, 1937, 1951, 5606	7
J25	25, 29, 1723, 1970, 1976, 1986, 1989, 1990, 1994, 2038, 2040, 2047, 2048, 2051, 2053, 2056, 2059, 2061, 2073, 2075, 2080, 2136, 2139, 5647, 5650, 5655, 5666, 5667, 5671, 5677, 5685, 5691, 5693, 5695, 5713, 5714, 5726	37
J26	412, 517, 1200, 1366, 1390, 1674	6
J27	917, 938, 1050, 1189, 2386, 2388, 2389, 2391	8
J28	2406, 2408, 2409, 2411, 2412, 2413, 2414, 2416, 2417, 2418, 2420, 2421, 2422, 2423, 2424, 2538, 2539, 2540, 2541, 2542	20
'398'	282, 1076	2
J39	1451, 1452, 1454, 1470, 1487, 1508, 1509, 1534, 4709, 4713, 4725, 4730, 4812, 4819, 4831, 4833, 4850, 4858, 4864, 4867, 4870, 4897, 4904, 4910, 4914, 4926, 4927, 4928, 4931, 4939, 4940, 4941, 4943, 4947, 4949, 4971, 4978	37
J71	27, 225, 239, 261, 272, 286, 299, 347, 448, 449, 451, 452, 493, 496, 499, 1083, 1084, 1155, 1199, 1789, 1797, 1864, 8230, 8251, 8264, 8281, 8284, 8298	28
J72	462, 512, 516, 524, 571, 574, 576, 1715, 1720, 1721, 1742, 1744, 2308, 2316, 2317, 2318, 8672, 8705, 8716, 8718, 8741, 8743, 8745, 8746, 69001, 69002, 69003, 69008, 69009, 69010, 69011, 69020	32
J73	545, 546, 549, 550, 551, 552	6
J74	20, 64, 82, 88, 461, 467, 489, 662	8
J75	2492, 2493, 2494, 2495, 2496, 2497, 2523, 2524, 2525, 2526, 2527, 2528, 2529, 2530, 2531, 2532	16
J76	171, 193, 598, 602, 1059	5
J77	145, 199, 614, 623, 948, 1340, 1341, 1433, 1461, 8401, 8402, 8409, 8414, 8425, 8440	15
J78	590	1
J80	2448, 2449, 2450	3
J94	68011, 68042	2
K3	53, 1100, 1106, 1108, 1119, 1304, 1307, 1322, 1324, 1339, 2427, 1813, 1814, 1818, 1844, 1846, 1847, 1854, 1857, 1869, 1871, 1872, 1874, 1875, 1883, 1884, 1892, 1893, 1897, 1901, 1904, 1922, 1927, 1930, 1945, 1952, 1962, 1965, 1969, 1985, 1986, 1987	42
K5	1863	1
L1	67719, 67721, 67727, 67728, 67730, 67736, 67754, 67755, 67759, 67763, 67764, 67765, 67766	13
N8	74, 76, 136, 210, 212, 215, 216, 218, 219, 261, 267, 284, 287, 293, 345, 346, 348, 351, 371, 373, 445, 503, 504, 509, 515, 523, 531, 535, 573, 683, 780, 856, 859, 860, 861, 862, 863, 864, 959, 961, 1072, 1091, 1104, 1105, 1124, 1127, 1152	47

Class	Number of engine when first allocated to Hull	Total

L.N.E.R. and B.R. types *cont.*

Class	Number of engine when first allocated to Hull	Total
N9	383, 1617, 1645, 1646, 1647, 1649, 1650, 1653, 1655, 1705	10
N10	89, 429, 1112, 1148, 1683, 1697, 1706, 1711, 1774, 1785, 9099, 9102, 9104, 9105, 9106	15
N11	2478, 2479, 2480, 2481, 2482	5
N12	2485, 2486, 2488, 2489, 2490, 2491	6
N13	2405, 2407, 2410, 2415, 2419, 2533, 2534, 2535, 2536, 2537	10
O1	6334, 6350, 6566, 6578, 6630, 3760, 3856	7
O4	5008, 5404, 6211, 6261, 6262, 6265, 6352, 6501, 6549, 6566, 6577, 6578, 6579, 6580, 6581, 6583, 6584, 6606, 6607, 6608, 6609, 6610, 6611, 6612, 6613, 6614, 6615, 6616, 6617, 6618, 6630, 6631, 6632, 3603, 3620, 3667, 3753	37
O7	3001, 3008, 3009, 3010, 3011, 3012, 3014, 3021, 3022, 3026, 3045, 3047, 3052, 3057, 3094, 3099, 3105, 3108, 3113, 3129, 3149, 3157, 3162, 3176, 90006, 90007, 90016, 90030, 90044, 90061, 90072, 90078, 90082, 90089, 90091, 90092, 90100, 90423, 90427, 90430, 90432, 90435, 90449, 90452, 90458, 90462, 90467, 90479, 90482, 90503, 90511	51
Q1	5087	1
Q5	130, 443, 578, 645, 652, 656, 659, 715, 764, 771, 773, 785, 1002, 1032, 1062, 1110, 1128, 1173, 1177, 1215, 1682, 1694	22
Q6	1247, 1249, 1257, 1262, 1276, 1280, 1284, 1291, 1292, 1311, 1361, 1362, 2217, 2218, 2219, 2220, 2221, 2223, 2224, 2226, 2227, 2228, 2229, 2230, 2231, 2233, 2234, 2235, 2237, 2239, 2241, 2242, 2243, 2244, 2246, 2247, 2248, 2249, 2250, 2251, 2252, 2254, 2255, 2257, 2261, 2264, 2270, 2272, 2273, 2275, 2277, 2278, 2283, 2287, 2291, 2294, 2297, 2299, 2301, 3395, 3431, 3437	62
Q7	624, 625, 626, 628, 629, 630, 901, 902, 904, 905	10
Q10	2498, 2499, 2500, 2501, 2502, 2503, 2504, 2505, 2506, 2507, 2508, 2509, 2510, 2511, 2512	15
T1	1350, 1352, 1356, 1657, 1658, 1660, 9914, 9918, 9921	9
V1/V3	7635, 7638, 7640, 7663, 7677, 7682, 7684, 7685, 7686, 7691	10
X2	957	1
X3	190	1
Y1	19, 79, 100, 106, 108, 187, 8145, 8148	8
Y3	90, 117, 148, 193, 8160, 8183	6
Y7	24, 900, 984, 985, 1302, 1798, 1799	7
Y8	559, 560, 561, 562, 563	5
WD	70834, 77004, 77032, 77055, 77067, 77075, 77128, 77138, 77149, 77167, 77218, 77248, 77338, 77353, 77445, 77468, 78553, 78601, 79182, 79243, 79280, 90116, 90160, 90172, 90210, 90213, 90217, 90233, 90235, 90240, 90262, 90265, 90272, 90352, 90378, 90382, 90409, 90567, 90571, 90586, 90609, 90623, 90627, 90661, 90663, 90670, 90674, 90677, 90688, 90695, 90704	51

Ex LMS types

Class	Number of engine when first allocated to Hull	Total
4MT	43015, 43038, 43053, 43069, 43076, 43077, 43078, 43079, 43096, 43099, 43100, 43101, 43102, 43103, 43122, 43123, 43124, 43125, 43126, 43127, 43128, 43130, 43131, 43138, 43141	25
3FT	47334, 47580, 47589, 47632	4
3MT	40012, 40017, 40045, 40056, 40057, 40059, 40060, 40061	8
2MT	41262	1
2MT	46409	1

BR Standards

Class	Number of engine when first allocated to Hull	Total
4MT	76022	1
3MT	77000, 77001, 77010	3
2MT	84009	1

Railcars

Class	Number of engine when first allocated to Hull	Total
Sentinel Steam	21, 22, 26, 29, 210, 212, 238, 244, 253, 254, 255, 263, 265, 267, 272, 273, 283, 2238, 2242, 2245, 2267	21
A.W. D/E	224, 232	2

B.R. Diesel Locomotives

Class	Number of engine when first allocated to Hull	Total
Cl.03	D2051, D2052, D2053, D2054, D2062, D2063, D2064, D2065, D2073, D2081, D2098, D2100, D2101, D2102, D2112, D2137, D2151, D2152, D2155, D2156, D2157, D2158, D2168, D2169, D2170, D2171, D2172, D2173, D2174	29
Cl.04	D2268	1
Cl.08	13070, 13071, 13072, 13073, 13074, 13075, 13076, 13077, 13078, 13079, 13080, 13081, 13137, 13138, 13139, 13142, 13143, 13230, 13231, 13232, 13233, 13234, 13235, 13236, D3313, D3318, D3323, D3675, D3676, D3734, D3944, D3945, 08004, 08008, 08093, 08099, 08177, 08296, 08304, 08317, 08386, 08391, 08392, 08435, 08440, 08499, 08567, 08745, 08885	49
Cl.11	12113, 12114, 12115, 12116, 12117, 12118, 12119, 12120, 12121, 12122	10
Cl.14	D9503, D9504, D9505, D9507, D9510, D9511, D9512, D9515, D9516, D9520, D9523, D9525, D9529, D9532, D9533, D9534, D9537, D9539, D9540, D9541, D9542, D9543, D9544, D9545, D9546, D9547, D9548, D9549, D9550, D9551, D9552, D9553, D9554	33
Cl.20	D8310, D8311, D8312, D8313, D8314, D8315	6
Cl.37	D6730, D6731, D6732, D6733, D6734, D6735, D6736, D6737, D6738, D6739, D6740, D6741, D6758, D6775, D6779, D6780, D6781, D6782, D6783, D6784, D6785, D6786, D6787, D6788, D6789, D6790, D6791, D6792, D6793, D6794, D6795, D6835, D6836	33
4WDM	56	1
	Total	1446

THE ENGINE SHEDS AT DAIRYCOATES

Some two miles to the west of Humber Dock, and then in the parish of Ferriby, was a large farm house and buildings by the name of Dairy Coates. Some of its land between the farmhouse and the River Humber foreshore was acquired in the late 1830's for the building of the Hull & Selby Railway, whose operation then deprived the farm of any easy access to the river. The extension of that railway, by a line from Hull to Bridlington in 1845, made the same kind of boundary to the east of the farm. Then in 1848, the farm became totally confined inside a triangle of lines when the Hull & Selby (by now the York & North Midland Railway) put in a line for its trains to be able to use Paragon instead of Manor House Street station as its Hull terminus. All three lines of the triangle saw a considerable increase of traffic in the 1850's, so how the farm fared, or even if it was still able to operate is problematical.

In 1857 it is no surprise that the North Eastern Railway's locomotive superintendent was reporting 'a great want of engine shed room at Hull', and that most of the engines based there had to stand out in the open. The only covered accommodation then provided was the 3-road straight shed in part of Paragon station for the passenger engines, and for the goods engines, one of similar size and style alongside Wellington Street between Manor House and Railway Streets. So Fletcher, along with the Company's

engineer, and the divisional engineer set about seeking a site for a shed of substantial size.

The large area at Dairy Coates Farm, encompassed by a triangle of lines must have been seen as an obvious, and very convenient answer to the problem, despite it then being so much 'out in the country'. Moves in that direction began in February 1858, but authorisation for it was not granted until March 1861, and what became No.1 shed opened in 1863, along with a fitting shop. The shed building was rectangular, but at its centre had a 42 foot turntable, with 18 tracks radiating from it, so the shed was actually termed a roundhouse. At a later date, the original turntable was replaced by one of 50 feet diameter.

Further covered housing for the engines was soon required and, starting in 1873, Nos.2 and 3 sheds were built, each with 20 roads radiating from the turntable which, if originally 42 feet, had been changed to 50 feet by the turn of the century. That size was certainly needed for the 0-8-0 engines built from 1901, which the shed got to haul the export coal traffic from South Yorkshire pits. Then from 1906 to 1912, Dairycoates began to take in 4-6-0 type engines (N.E.R. classes S and S2; LNER B13 & B15) which had a wheelbase of almost 51 feet and an overall length of 61 feet. From 1906 to 1909 it also took in, as assistant to the District Locomotive Superintendent and shedmaster, Edward

Thompson who became the LNER's controversial Chief Mechanical Engineer from 1941 to 1946. Not only were the engines getting bigger, but the number of them continued to increase year by year, general goods trains needed to be speeded up, and the 4-6-0's specialised on running fast fish trains. The three roundhouses gave nominal cover to no more than 60 engines, and one of our photographs, taken on a 1913 Sunday, shows more than that number having perforce had to be stabled outside the buildings. Obviously large scale extensions and improvements were imperative. They were actually authorised in 1911, but did not become fully effective until March 1916.

Three more, and larger, roundhouses were built, each equipped with a 60 feet diameter turntable, with 24 roads around each. All three turntables were inter-connected, and each roundhouse also had two access roads, on opposite sides of the building. These new sheds were also connected with the turntables in the three earlier sheds, each of which had a couple of access roads. Movement of engines within the sheds was thus minimised, and any derailment hitches could be readily circumvented. Additionally, a two-level building with parallel tracks was built to house a wheel-drop, hydraulically operated to and from the ground floor fitting shop. Along the south side of the new roundhouses, a separate single road straight shed

An incredible sight by any standards is this Sunday morning view of the south side of Dairycoates shed in 1913. Obviously posed - notice the whitened buffer and cylinder covers - the photograph is a graphic reminder of the how great our railways used to be. There are at least 64 locomotives in the picture, all facing west, and all except one are North Eastern engines, the odd one out is a Lancashire & Yorkshire Railway 0-8-0 which is second from left. This is Dairycoates before the three extra roundhouses were added on to the west end of the existing building, the coaling stage on the left being demolished to make way for the new sheds. *Authors collection.*

Raven S2 No.813 inside one of the new roundhouses about 1917. Built between 1911 and 1913, the twenty locomotives that comprised the class became Class B15 at Grouping but none became BR property. Although only two of the class were allocated to Dairycoates when the LNER came into being, most of them ended up there over the ensuing years and the fifteen survivors were working from the shed during the 1939-45 war years. *Authors collection.*

was added to house the breakdown train, with an uncluttered egress line, and the opportunity was taken to provide extensive stores, offices, and mess rooms.

The above catered for all requirements except that of providing the engines with coal, and for those based at Dairycoates, the individual capacities ranged from 4cwts on the 0-4-0 dock tanks to 5¹/₂ tons on the 0-8-0 mineral engines, and each day, about 150 engines needed replenishing. That objectionable, time and labour consuming job was completely off-set by the installation of the most advanced mechanical coaling plant in the country. Designed 'in-house' but erected by specialist contractors, and

electrically operated, it was indeed a landmark in both senses of that word. Two elevated bunkers took care of different grades of coal, and had a total capacity of 300 tons; each had two chutes positioned so that four engines could be coaled at the same time. It was first used on March 27th 1916, needed only one plant attendant and was so robust that it worked continuously for some 50 years. By 1966 the few steam engines still allocated to Dairycoates could be coaled by a JCB mobile hopper-loader, and in 1967, the awesome 'coal-cracker' (as it was locally known) was demolished.

Separate tabular information illustrates the importance of Dairycoates shed, and the number

of engines working from it, which dealt mainly with Hull's goods traffic. That is how it was generally regarded, but its mixed traffic engines, such as LNER classes B1, B16 and K3, regularly did passenger work, and up to the level of the Doncaster-Hull portion of the Yorkshire Pullman. At the other extreme were the five 0-4-0 dock tanks numbered 559 to 563, built in 1888 specifically for moving wagons of imported timber on Hull docks, where almost all of their 50 years working life was spent, apart from two notable exceptions. No.559 was entitled to medals for military service - in the 1914-18 war it worked at the Royal Arsenal, Woolwich, and in the Second World War spent

Nos.4, 5 and 6 sheds and associated offices in the course of erection in 1915. A local contractor was used for the job. Notice, to the left of the new offices, the redundant coal tubs from the former coal stage which stood approximately on the area occupied by the new No.4 roundhouse. *Authors collection.*

The steel clad coaling plant in 1962. Coal was raised to the upper bunkers by a series of small conveyor buckets fed from a sub surface bunker to where coal had been tipped direct from wagons. *The Rev.David Benson.*

1940-42 on the Spurn Head Railway helping the Royal Engineers build fortifications at the mouth of the river Humber. 561, 562 and 563 were scrapped in 1936/7 but the other two managed to dodge the drastic enemy bombing of Hull docks, and not until January 1945 was there no sign of at least one Y8 class at Dairycoates shed. At less then 18 feet long, they still had the authority and precedence to hold up road traffic at nine level crossings in the city as they made their leisurely way from (and to) Dairycoates in the west of the city, to their working place on Victoria Dock in the east of the city. The North Eastern Railway proved much too hasty in removing the shed which the Hull & Holderness Railway had erected in 1858, as it would have been an ideal home for them. With hindsight, it is incredible to appreciate how much money British Railways spent in the 1950's on the shed buildings at Dairycoates. Admittedly much of it was on necessary maintenance, an example of which was the £1335 authorised in 1953 for repairs to the asbestos smokejacks over the turntables in Nos. 3, 4, 5 and 6 sheds. That followed an interesting spending in 1951 of £550 on 'fixing smokeplates to

prevent engines blowing slates from the roof.' Maybe that was just a harbinger of what was to come, and an indication of how suspect was the roof of the whole shed, all of it then more than forty years old. In 1953 repairs had to be sanctioned for the roofs of the 1876 built Nos. 2 and 3 sheds, costing £1970 for the north span, £1790 for the south span, and £1815 for re-glazing the centre span roof. That of the still older

No.1 shed needed £880 for its north span, £1400 for the centre, and £790 for the south spans, plus £550 for the roof of the adjacent workshops. Even that expenditure was insignificant against what was begun in 1956.

For re-construction, and re-modelling, no less than £524,202 had to be authorised, and the extent of the work undertaken is shown in some of the illustrations. The existing roof over Nos. 2, 3, 4, 5 and 6 sheds was removed completely, and replaced by pre-cast concrete arches instead of iron-work to support the new one. No.6 shed was discarded, the wall across its west end was demolished, and a replacement was built across the west end of No.5. When work began in 1956, Dairycoates was still home to 106 locomotives, which had to find shelter, and avoid falling slate damage as best they could. Just to add to the inconvenience, in that year, £2480 was spent on repairs to the floors and rails surrounding Nos. 4 and 5 turntables, whilst in the yard the rebuilding of two hot ash pits each 120 feet long, and repairs to the other two cost another £4000. Even as late as 1960, there was still spending of £50,839 on that wholesale re-construction. The turntable and pits of the erstwhile No.6 shed had remained in use (in the open air) at least until after the 1962 summer but were then put out of use, the table removed, and the pits filled in. A June 1963 photograph shows they were disused. Only four years later steam locomotives also disappeared from Dairycoates, followed in September 1970 by complete closure for all locomotive purposes.

During the years 1935-39 and 1950-54 I spent many a pleasant Sunday afternoon wandering around the six turntables checking details for my Registers of LNER Locomotives, but as the switch to diesels waxed, so did my visits wane, ceasing altogether in 1954. In a previous joint

Demolition of the roundhouses in October 1956. With hindsight the massive expenditure to provide two new units seems somewhat wasteful when less than fifteen years later the sheds would be closed. *British Railways.*

A general view of Dairycoates shed in August 1962 with the 1916 coaling plant dominating the picture. Engines including a B1, a couple of WD's and an Ivatt Mogul are arranged around the outside No.6 turntable, whilst a K3 and another of the ubiquitous WD 2-8-0s stand at the coaler. The lofty roof of the rebuilt engine shed, formerly Nos.4 and 5 sheds, is apparent. *Authors collection.*

book with Mick Nicholson on Hull's Railways *Irwell Press 1993*, we remarked on what we understood to be the position at Dairycoates in 1993, so to provide an up-date, a visit was made at the end of November 1994. Nos. 1, 2 and 3 sheds have gone completely, but what were Nos. 4 and 5 are in excellent use for warehousing goods of wide variety in course of both export and import. Their storage is immaculately arranged in an atmosphere that is almost clinical, and the smells and signs of coal smoke and diesel fuel have been exorcised without any trace. Greenpeace could very happily hold an annual conference or general meeting there. Sadly, to me, the tremendous amount of in-and-out traffic was entirely by road.

However, the visit was not entirely without cheer. Turning our car about at the site of what was Dairycoates signalbox, we paused to study a road warning sign at an unguarded level crossing of just a single line of railway track which showed evidence that it was still used, and to twist the knife, the warning signs depict a reasonable drawing of a 4-6-0 steam locomotive belching smoke. Whilst there, completely by chance, from under the adjacent Priory Yard overbridge (which still carries our passenger trains to Leeds and to Doncaster) came a Class 60 diesel locomotive named JOSEPH BANKS at a steady walking pace, hauling 24 of the very latest design wagons fully loaded with roadstone aggregate. It was the regular Tilcon train from the Skipton area quarries to the distribution plant which now occupies part of where Outwards Yard used to be. It must have been every ounce of a thousand-ton load, and the kind of business for which British Railways are best suited, but here, in Hull, we were treated to an experience that is common-place, and taken for granted in the United States and Canada. So what was the round-the-clock activity and workplace of thousands of Hull railwaymen, still has frequent passenger trains on one side of it, and regular mineral trains on the other side, and we came away from its morbid site much encouraged.

Back in steam days, no V2 class 2-6-2, nor any of the 4-6-2 classes was ever allocated to Dairycoates, but from 1964 to 1967, the sidings adjacent to Dairycoates shed were the temporary resting place of no less than 732 steam

An unidentified V3 and B12 No.61577 occupy two of the radiating roads around the now exposed No.3 turntable in May 1959. A B12 was something of a rarity in Hull and this example only ended up at Dairycoates because it had developed a hot axlebox whilst hauling an excursion from Lincoln to Bridlington and had been brought to the shed for repair on the 14th May. After the axlebox had been relined the engine spent a couple of days in the area doing local trips to give the axle time to bed in after which the locomotive returned to its home shed at Cambridge on the 21st May. No.2 turntable, nearest the camera, along with No.3, was once covered by the sheds built in 1876, the original 42 ft turntables being enlarged, shortly after 1900, to 50 ft diameter. *Peter Harrod*

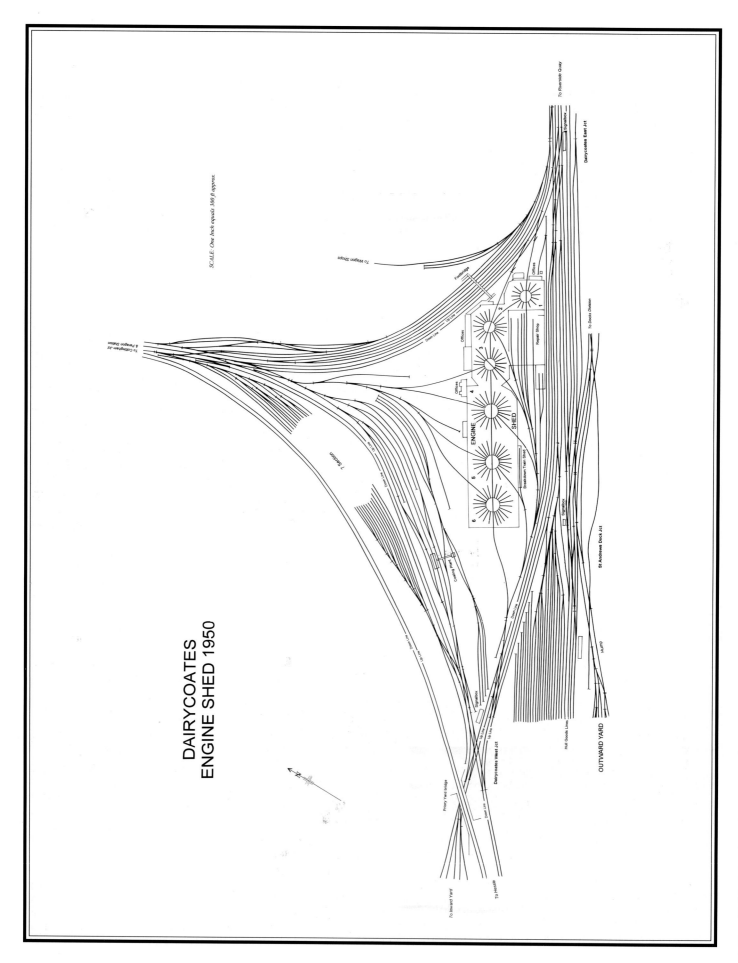

DAIRYCOATES
ENGINE SHED 1950

SCALE: One Inch equals 300 ft approx.

locomotives, including eight class A3 (60036/ 45/70/71/80/85/91/92), ten Peppercorn class A1 (60124/6/8/40/1/3/5/7/50/57), and also two V2's 60831 and 60961. They were then hauled - as required - to be cut up in the scrap yard that Albert Draper & Son Ltd had established in the former Hull & Barnsley goods yard at Sculcoates. Enthusiasts will notice that (apart from the preserved 4771 Green Arrow) the last surviving V2 was among them, and also the final A1 No.60145 SAINT MUNGO, about which such a fuss has recently been made anent the construction of a successor to that class, to become 60163 TORNADO. Once again the saddest words are 'If only....' and what a tremendous amount of money, effort, argument, and printed space could have been saved *IF ONLY* the late Albert Draper had thought more of 60145 than of LMS 'Black Five' 5303, now restored to running condition and bearing his name. Preserved Black Fives are almost ten-a-penny; an original Peppercorn A1 would now have been almost priceless.

(below) **Worsdell NER 4-4-0 Class R No.1223 alongside the south entrance to Dairycoates No.3 roundhouse circa 1920. Each of the six round-houses had at least three entrance/exit roads, Nos.2, 3, 4 and 5 sheds had four each. Including those roads as stabling too, each of the sheds had radiating roads as follows: No.1 - 18, Nos. 2 and 3 - 20, Nos.4, 5 and 6 - 24 roads. From 1922 to June 1959 no 4-4-0 type locomotive was allocated to Dairycoates although they did continue to call there for servicing after working into the city.** *Real Photos.*

(above) **The western elevation of the rebuilt No.5 shed in June 1963 with the exposed No.6 turntable in front. On the extreme right is the single road, breakdown train shed, which survived the 1950s rebuilding unaltered and is still standing today although now in private hands.** *(below)* **One of the heavy Tilcon aggregate trains alongside the remains of Dairycoates shed. This late June 1993 view shows one of the latest BR Class 60 diesel electric locomotives, 60084 CROSS FELL, waiting to reverse its 1,000 ton plus load into the Tilcon construction materials plant.** *Tony Buckton.*

HULL DAIRYCOATES

Allocation as at 1st January 1923:-

A7 1126, 1175
B13 726, 740, 744, 746, 748, 749, 751, 755, 758, 760, 763, 2004, 2009, 2010
B15 786, 815
E5 1468
J21 86, 97, 102, 291, 294, 316, 331, 431, 665, 680, 778, 810, 874, 963, 976, 981, 993, 1513, 1548, 1568, 1571, 1572, 1590, 1612, 1845
J22 422, 571
J25 2038, 2048
'398' 282, 1076
J71 448, 1083, 1155, 1199, 1864
J72 462, 1715, 1721, 2308, 2317, 2318
J76 193, 598, 602, 1059
J77 145, 199, 623, 948, 1349, 1433, 1461
N8 74, 76, 210, 215, 216, 219, 284, 287, 346, 373, 509, 515, 523, 531, 535, 573, 683, 861, 864, 959, 1124
N9 1647
N10 89, 1112, 1697, 1706, 1711, 1774, 1785
Q5 130, 443, 645, 652, 669, 715, 771, 773, 785, 1002, 1062, 1173, 1177, 1215, 1682, 1694
Q6 2217, 2218, 2220, 2221, 2233, 2234, 2239, 2241, 2244, 2246, 2249, 2250, 2252, 2270, 2272, 2278, 2297, 2301
Q7 901, 902, 904, 905
T1 1350, 1352
Y8 559, 560, 561, 562, 563

Subsequent changes to the allocation up to 1970 were as follows:-

1923	IN	B15 782; J25 2047, 2051; J27 917; J71 261; J72 1744; Q6 1291 (7)
	OUT	J25 2047; Q6 2234, 2301 (3)
1924	IN	B13 747, 2001, 2003; J27 2386; N10 1148; Q5 764; Q6 2234; Q7 624, 625, 626, 628, 629, 630 (13)
	OUT	B13 746; E5 1468; J21 431, 874; J22 422, 571; J25 2038, 2051; J27 917; '398' 282; J72 462; Q5 443, 645, 785, 1002, 1062; Q6 2233, 2252 (18)
1925	IN	B14 2111, 2112, 2113, 2114; B16 1384; J21 431; J71 451; J72 524, 571; N8 76, 351; N9 1653; Q5 443, 652, 656, 785, 1128 (17)
	OUT	B13 744; J21 86, 291, 431; J25 2048; J27 2386; J71 1155; J72 1744, 2308; J76 193, 598, 602, 1059; N8 76; Q5 652, 715, 1173; Q6 2249 (18)
1926	IN	J39 1451, 1452, 1454; J71 1789; J72 574; N8 861, 1104; Q5 1110; Q6 2233; 2249; T1 1660 (11)
	OUT	N8 861, 1104; Q7 629, 902 (4)
1927	IN	B13 756; B16 925; J21 86, 291, 564, 874; J23 2521; N8 351, 373; N9 1617, 1649, 1650; N11 2480, 2482; N12 2488; O4 6607, 6610, 6611, 6616; Q6 1247, 2223, 2229, 2264; Q10 2501, 2502; Y3 90 (26)
	OUT	J21 1568; J39 1451, 1452, 1454; N8 351, 373; N12 2488; Q5 669, 785, 1110; Q6 1291 (11)
1928	IN	B13 738, 744, 757; B14 2115; B16 936, 942; J27 1189; J28 2408, 2416; N10 429; O4 6577, 6578, 6581, 6583, 6584, 6608, 6609, 6612, 6613, 6614, 6615, 6618, 6630, 6632 (24)
	OUT	B13 2004; '398' 1076; O4 6610, 6611; Q5 443, 1128, 1682, 1694; Q7 624, 625, 626, 628, 630, 901, 904, 905; Q10 2501, 2502 (18)
1929	IN	B15 788, 823; B16 909, 928, 933, 1371, 1374, 1375, 1376, 1378, 2380; J72 462; N8 371; N11 2479; Q6 1362, 2224, 2226, 2251, 2273, 2283; Q10 2500, 2501, 2510, 2512; Y1 106, 108; Y3 193 (27)
	OUT	B13 763, 768; B14 2111, 2115; J27 1189; J77 623; N8 861; O4 6577, 6578, 6581, 6584, 6609, 6612, 6613, 6614, 6615, 6618; Y1 108 (18)
1930	IN	B16 840, 841, 842, 1385; J28 2413, 2420; N11 2478; Q6 1276, 1361, 2248, 2255; Q10 2503, 2511; T1 1657 (14)
	OUT	B13 749, 758; B14 2113, 2114; J21 86; N8 74, 351; N11 2479; O4 6583, 6607, 6608, 6616, 6630, 6632; Q10 2503; T1 1660 (16)
1931	IN	B16 930, 934, 937, 2367, 2369, 2379; J26 517, 1674; T1 1658, 1660; Y1 187; Y3 148 (12)
	OUT	B13 744, 760, 2001, 2003, 2009, 2010; B14 2112; J21 810; J77 145, 199, 948, 1349; N8 216, 371; Q5 130, 652, 656, 771, 1177, 1215; Q10 2500, 2501, 2510, 2511, 2512; Y3 148 (26)
1932	IN	A7 1170, 1179, 1195; J72 1720; J77 199, 948, 1349; Q5 652, 656, 771, 1177, 1215; Y1 106 (13)
	OUT	B13 740, 747, 757; J23 2521; Y1 106 (5)
1933	IN	J28 2411, 2412, 2414, 2417, 2418, 2540, 2541; O4 6580, 6615 (9)
	OUT	J21 102, 294, 665, 778, 963, 1513; N8 373; N11 2482; Q5 773; Q6 2218, 2223, 2249 (12)
1934	IN	B16 843, 846, 906; J12 875, 1558; J23 2441, 2445, 2452, 2456, 2462, 2464; J28 2421, 2422, 2423, 2424, 2538, 2539, 2542; J71 272,

1934 OUT cont
299; J77 145; N8 218, 860 (23)

	OUT	B13 755, 756; J21 564, 680; J28 2417; J77 1349; Q5 652, 656, 771, 1177; N8 76, 210, 959 (13)
1935	IN	B13 753; J21 613, 1556; J23 2475; J24 1931; J25 25, 2059; J28 2406, 2409; N12 2488; T1 1356 (11)
	OUT	A7 1179; J21 316, 331, 613, 875, 1548, 1558, 1815; J23 2445; Q5 764, 1215; Y3 193 (12)
1936	IN	B16 922; J21 568, 876, 1805; J23 2469; J25 1970, 1990, 2136; N10 1683; N11 2479 (10)
	OUT	B13 726, 751; J21 981, 1571, 1572; J23 2441; N8 284; N12 2488; O4 6580; Q6 1247, 2224, 2233, 2273; Y8 561 (14)
1937	IN	A6 686, 688, 690; A7 1113, 1179; B13 759; B15 817; B16 943, 1373, 2365, 2377; J21 139, 312, 875, 1510, 1516, 1552, 1554, 1810; J23 2441; J25 2080; J39 1470, 1487, 1508; J72 2316; J77 614; N8 212, 271, 504, 862; N9 383; Q6 1262 (32)
	OUT	B15 786, 788; J21 291, 1612; J23 2441, 2452, 2456, 2462, 2464, 2469, 2475; J24 1931; J25 1970; J28 2406, 2408, 2409, 2411, 2412, 2414, 2416, 2418, 2420, 2421, 2422, 2423, 2538, 2539, 2540, 2541, 2542; J71 448, 451, 1083, 1199, 1864; J72 1720, 1721; J77 145, 199, 614, 948, 1433; N8 215, 287, 504, 509, 523, 531, 860; N10 89, 429, 1711; O4 6615; Q6 2239; Y8 562, 563 (57)
1938	IN	A7 1114; J21 122, 665, 1595; J26 1390; J27 1050; J39 1509, 1534 (8)
	OUT	A6 686, 688, 690; B13 738, 748, 753, 759; J21 122, 568, 874, 875; J25 2059, 2080; J28 2413; J39 1534; N9 1650 (16)
1939	IN	A7 1182, 1185, 1191; B15 795, 796, 798, 825; J26 412, 1200, 1366; J71 239, 286, 449, 452, 493, 1083, 1084, 1797, 1864; J77 623; N8 74, 293, 503, 780, 863, 961, 1072, 1091, 1105, 1127, 1132; N9 1645, 1646, 1655, 1705; Q6 2219, 2249, 2261, 2287, 2291; Y1 79; Y7 984, 985 (43)
	OUT	B16 925, 934, 1373, 2379; J21 97, 1510, 1516; J25 25, 1990, 2136; J71 493; J72 462, 524, 571, 574, 1715, 2316, 2317, 2318; J77 623, 1461; N8 535, 683, 863, 961, 1124; N10 1112, 1148, 1683, 1697, 1706, 1774, 1785; N11 2478, 2479, 2480; Q6 2221, 2248, 2249, 2272; T1 1350; Y7 984, 985 (43)
1940	IN	B15 820, 821 (2)
	OUT	A7 1114, 1126, 1195; B15 796; B16 843, 922, 928, 942, 943, 1371, 1375, 1385, 2369; J21 976; J26 412, 517, 1200, 1366, J27 1050; J39 1470; J71 299, 449; N9 1646, 1655; Q6 1262, 1362, 2217, 2220, 2229, 2234, 2244, 2250, 2261, 2264, 2283, 2291 (36)
1941	IN	B16 1382 (1)
	OUT	B16 906; Y1 106 (2)
1942	IN	J72 1721, 1744; J77 1341; N9 1646; Y1 19, 100 (6)
	OUT	B16 933; J21 1810; J71 239, 272; T1 1657; Y1 187; Y3 90; Y8 559 (8)
1943	IN	B15 787, 796, 813, 819, 822, 824; C6 699, 701, 703, 1794; C7 709, 710, 718, 722, 733, 2168, 2169, 2170, 2172, 2195, 2196, 2198, 2199, 2201, 2203, 2204, 2206, 2207, 2208, 2209, 2211, 2212; J21 613, 973, 1510, 1552, 1556, 1589, 1591, 1810; J24 1860, 1891; N8 136, 210, 345, 535, 856, 859, 863, 961; Q6 2234, 2275, 2291; Y8 559 (54)
	OUT	B16 840, 841, 842, 846, 909, 930, 936, 937, 1374, 1376, 1378, 1382, 1384, 2365, 2367, 2377, 2380; C7 2169, 2170, 2198, 2199, 2212; J21 139, 876, 993, 1552, 1554, 1556, 1590, 1595, 1805; J26 1390, 1674; J39 1487, 1508, 1509; J77 1341; N8 218; N9 383, 1617, 1645, 1646, 1647, 1649, 1653, 1705; Q6 1276, 2219, 2241; Y8 560 (50)
1944	IN	C6 696, 697, 698, 702, 742, 1753; C7 736, 2165; J21 123; J24 1891, 1892; J25 1723; Q1 5087; Q6 1257, 1276, 2219, 2228, 2235, 2241, 2242, 2278 (21)
	OUT	A7 1113; B15 813, 822, 823, 825; C6 699, 701, 1794; C7 710, 2172, 2204, 2206, 2208, 2209; J24 1860, 1891; Q1 5087; Q6 2246, 2251, 2278, 2287 (21)
1945	IN	A7 1113, 1129, 1190; F4 7578; J24 1860; K3 53, 1100, 1106, 1304, 1307, 1322, 1324, 1339, 2427; O1 6350, 6566; O4 6265, 6584, 6608, 6612 (20)
	OUT	B15 795, 796, 798; C6 697, 703; C7 722, 733, 2168, 2196, 2207, 2211; F4 7578; J25 1723; Q6 1257, 1361, 2226, 2235, 2270, 2278, 2297; Y8 559 (21)
1946	IN	A7 9772, 9778, 9780, 9783, 9788; C7 720; F4 7175, 7184; J21 5041; J24 1937, 1951; J25 5647, 5651, 5660, 5663, 5666, 5668, 5671, 5679, 5690, 5698, 5699, 5705, 5712, 5713; K3 1871, 1874, 1922; K5 1863; O4 3628, 3664, 3764, 3772, 3816, 3855; Q6 3403, 3408, 3444 (38)
	OUT	B15 782, 787, 817, 819, 821, 824; C6 702, 1753; C7 709, 718, 736; J21 123, 312, 613, 665, 973, 1510, 1552, 1556, 1589, 1591; O1 6350, 6566 (23)
1947	IN	C7 2970, 2982, 2983, 2995; F4 7171; J39 4867, 4914; K3 1813,

1814, 1872, 1883, 1892, 1903, 1927, 1945, 1965; N10 9094, 9096, 9098, 9104, 9108; WD 70834, 77032, 77248, 78532, 78553, 78578, 78585, 78614, 79186, 79209, 79239, 79243 (33)

OUT   B15 815, 820; C6 696, 698; C7 720, 2165, 2195, 2201; F4 7175; J21 1810, 5041; J24 1891; J25 5668; K5 1863; N8 136, 210, 212, 345, 863; Q6 1276, 2219, 2228, 2234, 2241, 2242, 2255, 2275, 2291, 3403, 3408, 3444 (31)

1948 IN   B1 1060, 1068, 1074, 1080; J21 5027, 5029, 5030, 5037, 5056, 5086, 5102; J24 5606; J39 4864, 4870, 4897, 4926, 4927, 4928, 4931, 4939, 4941, 4978; N8 9376, 9398; N10 9105, 9106; O7 3014, 3021, 3022, 3026 (30)

OUT   C6 742; C7 2203, 2970, 2982, 2983, 2995; J21 5027, 5056; J24 1860, 1892, 1937, 1951; J25 5660, 5671, 5679; N8 856, 961, 1091; WD 70834, 77032, 78553, 79243, 90208, 90378, 90382, 90403, 90409, 90663, 90677, 90695 * (22)

1949 IN   J21 5026, 5112; J25 5654, 5707; J71 8296, 8298; J72 8748, 69010, 69011; J77 8401; N10 9093, 9099, 9102, 9105, 9107; O1 3676, 3712, 3740, 3760, 3856, 3874; Q6 3348, 3358, 3395, 3431, 3437, 3448; O4 3603, 3673, 3732, 3753, 3754, 3769, 3828, 3835, 3845, 3849, 3857; O7 90006, 90008, 90009, 90011, 90021, 9026, 90057, 90450, 90478, 90483; WD 90272, 90309, 90378, 90382, 90394, 90409, 90526, 90571, 90661, 90663, 90677, 90688, 90695; T1 9914 (62)

OUT   J21 5026, 5029, 5037, 5086, 5112; J24 5606; J25 5705; J39 4978; J72 1721, 1744; N8 74, 271, 346, 503, 780; N10 9105; O4 3673, 3752, 3754, 3849; O7 3014, 3021, 3026; Q6 3348, 3358, 3395, 3431, 3437, 3448; WD 90208, 90378, 90382, 90394, 90403, 90409, 90526, 90663, 90677, 90695 (39)

1950 IN   A7 9771; J39 4910; O4 3673, 3732, 3754; O7 90007, 90047, 90435, 90470; WD 90160, 90217, 90378, 90567, 90586, 90704; LM4 43053, 43076, 43077, 43078, 43079 (20)

OUT   J21 5030, 5102; J25 5651, 5666, 5698, 5707, 5712; J39 4864, 4870, 4897, 4910, 4931, 4939; J71 452, 1084; N8 515, 535, 9376; N10 9105; O4 6612, 3845, 3857; O7 90011, 90026, 90470, 90478; T1 1658; WD 90217, 90272, 90309, 90378, 90382, 90571, 90586, 90661, 90677, 90688, 90695 (38)

1951 IN   J39 4713, 4725, 4730; J72 8673; K3 1844, 1846, 1847, 1869, 1893; O4 3620, 3843; O7 90001, 90022, 90030, 90061, 90072, 90078, 90089, 90099, 90423, 90427, 90430, 90432, 90449, 90450, 90458, 90479, 90482; T1 9919; WD 90210, 90233, 90235, 90272, 90352, 90382, 90609, 90627, 90674, 90695, 90704; Y3 8183; LM4 43099, 43100, 43101, 43102, 43103, 43122, 43124, 43125, 43126, 43127, 43128, 43130, 43131 (54)

OUT   A7 1185, 9780; F4 7171, 7184; J25 5647, 5654, 5663, 5690, 5699, 5713; J39 4730, 4867, 4926, 4927, 4941; J71 1789; J72 8673, 8748; N8 293, 9398; O1 3676, 3712, 3740, 3760, 3856, 3874; O4 3603, 3620, 3628, 3664, 3673, 3732, 3753, 3754, 3764, 3769, 3772, 3816, 3828, 3835, 3843, 3855, 6265, 6584, 6608; O7 90001, 90022, 90427, 90450, 90483; T1 1356; WD 90233, 90663, 90704; Y1 19; LM4 43125, 43126, 43128 (58)

1952 IN   J39 4703, 4904, 4947, 4971; WD 90623; LM4 43015, 43038, 43069;

BR4 76022; DES 12113, 12114, 12115, 12116, 12117, 12118, 12119, 12120, 12121, 12122 (19)

OUT   A7 1170, 1175, 9783; J39 4703, 4713, 4904, 4928; K3 1899, 1927, 1932; N8 219, 862, 1072, 1105; O7 90007, 90423, 90432, 90435, 90449; T1 1352, 1660, 9914, 9919; WD 90235, 90567, 90623, 90674; LM4 43101, 43102, 43127 (30)

1953 IN   A7 9781; J71 8281, 8284; J72 8743, 8747; J77 8402, 8413; K3 1884; DES 13071, 13072, 13073, 13074, 13075 (13)

OUT   J71 1864, 8281, 8284; J72 69010 69011; J77 8413; N8 573, 859; O7 90047; Y1 79; DES 12113, 12114, 12115, 12116 (14)

1954 IN   J39 4819, 4864, 4904, 4949; J71 8284; J72 8670, 8741, 8751, 8753; J77 8429; Y1 8148, 8151; Y3 8182; DES 13070, 13076, 13077, 13078, 13079, 13080, 13081 (20)

OUT   A7 1113, 1179, 9771, 9778, 9781; B1 1068; J39 4725, 4904, 4947; J71 1797; J72 8743, 8747; J77 8401, 8402, 8429; N8 1152; O7 90061; Y1 100, 8151; DES 12117, 12118, 12119, 12120, 13071, 13072 (25)

1955 IN   J25 5655, 5693, 5695, 5726; J71 8230; K3 1899, 1904, 1932; Y1 8145; Y3 8160; DES 13071, 13072, 13137, 13138, 13139, 13142, 13143, 13230, 13231 (19)

OUT   A7 1129, 1182, 1190, 9772, 9778; J71 286, 8284; N8 864, 1127; N10 9093, 9098, 9102, 9106; O7 90021; WD 90210, 90352, 90409; Y1 8148; Y3 8183; LM4 43015, 43038, 43122, 43124, 43130; DES 12121, 12122, 13137, 13138, 13139 (29)

1956 IN   J25 5677; J39 4910, 4939, 4940; O7 90100; WD 90670; LM4 43122; DES 13232, 13233, 13234, 13235, 13236, 13323 (13)

OUT   A7 1191; K3 1844, 1869; O7 90482; WD 90378; Y1 8145; Y3 8160, 8182; BR4 76022; DES 13142, 13232, 13233, 13234, 13235, 13236 (15)

1957 IN   J25 5654, 5663, 5685, 5691; J71 8251, 8264; J72 8672, 8746, 8752; J94 8042; K3 1854, 1857, 1897; T1 9918, 9921 (15)

OUT   B1 1060, 1074, 1080; J25 5663, 5685, 5695; J39 4864, 4939, 4949; J71 261, 1083, 8298; J72 8672, 8741; N10 9094, 9096, 9107, 9108; O7 90089, 90100; T1 9918, 9921; WD 90378 (23)

1958 IN   B1 1065, 1256; G5 7341; J39 4947; J72 69008; J73 8360, 8361; J77 8409, 8414, 8425; J94 8011; O7 90011, 90427, 90482, 90503, 90511; WD 90217, 90233, 90352, 90378, 90571, 90586, 90623, 90677, 90688, 90378, 90677; BR3 77000, 77010; DES 13232 (30)

OUT   J25 5654, 5677, 5726; G5 7341; J71 8256; J72 8746; J77 8414; K3 1854, 1884, 1923, 1934; N10 9099, 9104; O7 90430, 90479; WD 90378, 90677; DES 13143 (18)

1959 IN   B1 1010, 1215, 1289, 61306; D49 2701, 2707, 2710, 2717, 2720, 2722, 2723, 2727, 2740, 2759, 2760, 2763, 2765; J39 4831, 4833, 4904, 4943; J72 8672, 8746, 8752; J73 8363; V1/V3 7635, 7638, 7640, 7643, 7677, 7682, 7684, 7686; LM4 43123; BR3 77001; BR2 84009:DM 2051, 2052, 2053, 2054 (40)

OUT   D49 2701, 2707, 2720, 2722, 2760; J25 5655; J71 8251; J72 8741, 8751; J73 8363; J77 8409; O7 90011, 90057; WD 90233, 90704; LM4 43053, 43099, 43100, 43103, 43122 (20)

1960 IN   B1 1012, 61305; J72 8673, 8716, 8745, 69009, 69010, 69011,

An unidentified Class K (later LNER Class Y8) at work in the Victoria dock at about the turn of the century. There were only five locomotives in the class, all built in June 1890 at Gateshead specifically to work the considerable timber traffic passing through Hull's docks. All five were still stationed at Dairycoates at Grouping but during the LNER period they spent much of their lives in store due to lack of work in trade depressions. By June 1937 there were only two engines surviving, 559 and 560, and during World War Two these left Dairycoates, the latter never to return. *Authors collection.*

1960 IN cont

69020; K3 1869, 1875, 1901, 1923, 1927, 1985; LM2 41262;
LM3F 47334, 47580, 47589, 47632; DES 13233, D3675, D3676,
D3944, D3945; DM 2064, 2151, 2168, 2169, 2170, 2171, 2172, 2173,
2174, 2268 (35)

OUT   D49 2710, 2740; J25 5691; J39 4910, 4947; J71 8230, 8264;
J72 8670, 8705, 8752, 8753, 69008; J73 8360, 8361; J77 8425;
O7 90022, 90072, 90503, 90511; WD 90160; LM3F 47589;
DES 13070, 13071 (23)

1961 IN   K3 1818, 1854, 1884, 1906, 1952, 1986, 1987; LM4 43096;
D17/3 6730, 6731 (10)

OUT   D49 2717, 2723, 2727, 2759, 2763, 2765; J25 5693; J39 4831, 4833,
4904, 4914; J72 8672, 8673, 8716, 8745; J94 8011; K3 1814, 1874,
1892, 1901, 1902, 1903, 1904, 1920, 1927, 1941; O7 90030, 90078;
V3 7635, 7640, 7682; WD 90217, 90571, 90623; LM3F 47334,
47580, 47632; DES 13072, 13073, 13076, 13078; DM 2151,
2268 (43)

1962 IN   B1 1255, 1303; B16 1418, 1420, 1435, 1437, 1438, 1444, 1453,
1463, 1467, 61472; J39 4850; K3 1930, 1962, 1969; O7 90435;
DES 12122, D3234, D3236, D3318; DM 2268; D17/3 6732, 6733,
6734, 6735, 6736, 6737, 6738, 6739, 6740, 6741, 6779, 6780, 6781,
6782, 6783 (37)

OUT   B1 1215; B16 1420; J39 4819, 4850, 4940, 4943, 4971; J72 69010,
69020; K3 1813, 1818, 1819, 1846, 1847, 1854, 1857, 1869, 1871,
1872, 1875, 1883, 1884, 1893, 1897, 1899, 1906, 1922, 1923, 1930,
1932, 1933, 1945, 1952, 1962, 1965, 1969, 1985, 1986, 1987;
V3 7677; LM4 43096; BR2 84009; DM 2051, 2170, 2173, 2174,
2268 (47)

1963 IN   B1 1032, 1176; B16 61475; O7 90044, 90057, 90091, 90092, 90452,
90462, 90478; WD 90262, 90265, 90704; DES 12113, 12114, 12115,
12116, 12117, 12118, 12119, 12120, 12121, D3235; DM 2081, 2098,
2101, 2102, 2155, 2156, 2157 (30)

OUT   B1 61305; B16 61475; J72 69009, 69011; J94 8042; O7 90006,
90091, 90092, 90099, 90427, 90435; V3 7638, 7643, 7684, 7686;
WD 90609; LM2 41262; LM4 43131; BR3 77000, 77001, 77010;
DES D3230, D3231, D3235; D17/3 6780, 6781, 6782, 6783 (28)

1964 IN   O7 90092; WD 90213; LM4 43138, 43141; DES D3070, D3071,
D3313; DM 2065; D17/3 6758, 6775, 6781, 6782, 6783 (13)

OUT   B1 1065, 1176, 1256, 1303; B16 1418, 1435, 1437, 1438, 1444,
1453, 1463, 1467, 61472; O7 90482; LM4 43138, 43141; DM 2054,
2065; D17/3 6779 (19)

1965 IN   B1 1002, 61322; O7 90030; WD 90240 (4)

OUT   B1 1010; O7 90030, 90092, 90452; LM4 43069, 43076, 43077,
43078, 43079; DES D3071; DM 2081 (11)

1966 IN   O7 90016, 90479; DM 2100; D17/3 6835, 6836; CL14 D9503,
D9504, D9505, D9512, D9515, D9516, D9520, D9523, D9525,
D9541, D9542, D9546, D9547, D9548, D9549, D9550, D9551,
D9552, D9553, D9554 (25)

OUT   B1 1012, 1032, 61322; O7 90016, 90044, 90057, 90479; WD 90213,
90586, 90704; LM4 43123; DM 2052, 2053 (13)

1967 IN   DM 2155, 2170, 2174; D17/3 6784, 6785, 6786, 6787, 6788, 6789,
6790, 6791, 6792, 6793, 6794, 6795; CL14 D9507, D9510, D9511,
D9529, D9532, D9533, D9534, D9537, D9539, D9540, D9543,
D9544, D9545 (28)

OUT   B1 1002, 1255, 1289, 61306; O7 90008, 90009, 90450, 90458,
90462, 90478; WD 90240, 90262, 90265, 90272, 90352, 90627,
90670, 90677, 90688, 90695; DES 12113; DM 2101, 2102, 2155;
D17/3 6785, 6786, 6787 (28)

1968 IN   CL20 8310, 8311, 8312, 8313, 8314, 8315 (6)

OUT   DES 12117, 12118, 12119, 12120; DM 2098, 2155, 2156, 2157,
2169, 2170; D17/3 6758, 6775, 6791, 6792, 6793, 6794, 6795;
CL14 D9503, D9504, D9505, D9507, D9510, D9511, D9512, D9515,
D9516, D9520, D9523, D9525, D9529, D9532, D9533, D9534,
D9537, D9539, D9540, D9541, D9542, D9543, D9544, D9545,
D9546, D9547, D9548, D9549, D9550, D9551, D9552, D9553,
D9554 (50)

1969 IN   DM 2062 (1)

OUT   DES 12116, 12122; DM 2062, 2064; D17/3 6730, 6731, 6732, 6733,
6734, 6735, 6736, 6737, 6738, 6739, 6740, 6741, 6781, 6782, 6783,
6784, 6788, 6789, 6790, 6835, 6836; CL20 8310, 8311, 8312, 8313,
8314, 8315 (31)

1970 IN   (0)

OUT   DES 3070, 3074, 3075, 3077, 3079, 3080, 3081, 3232, 3233, 3234,
3236, 3313, 3318, 3323, 3675, 3676, 3944, 3945, 12114, 12115,
12121; DM 2100, 2168, 2171, 2172, 2174 (26)

* These eight WD 2-8-0s were renumbered.

Y8 8090, alias NER 559, inside one of the Dairycoates roundhouses in April 1947. The engine was only visiting for a repair beyond the capabilities of its new shed Springhead. Compared with the previous picture 8090 has gained a new boiler, the former 'marine type' boiler having been discarded in about 1904. Just over a year later 8090 moved north to Tyneside ending all Y8 links with Hull. *H.C.Casserley.*

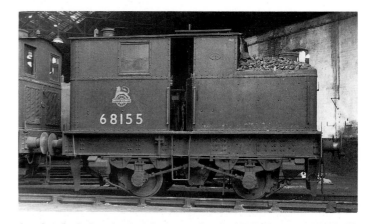

Another dock shunting type long associated with Hull was the LNER Y3 Sentinels. Here 68155 resides in one of Dairycoates sheds with another member of the class in March 1953. *R.J.Buckley.*

A visiting GCR built O5 2-8-0 No.5013 in Dairycoates yard on 19th October 1935 after having worked in on a goods train from the Sheffield area. The very similar Class O4 (the difference in the classes was mainly the size of boilers, the O5 had a larger boiler) were well known in Hull with both Dairycoates and Springhead sheds having allocations during the LNER and BR periods. *Mrs.A.Yeadon's Brownie camera.*

LNER C7 No.2988 outside the straight shed at Dairycoates in June 1946. The Raven designed Z Class Atlantic had previously been 2203 but in the LNER renumbering scheme of 1946 it was brought into line with all the remaining members of the class in the number group 2950 - 2997, although not all of the surviving engines of the once fifty strong class were renumbered. It was built in 1915 at Darlington and was withdrawn in July 1948 before it had 60,000 added to its number by British Railways. Comparative strangers to the Hull area before the second war, no less than twenty two C7's were working from Dairycoates by 1943. This view also depicts some interesting aspects of the engine shed which besides showing the west (open end) elevation of the 5-road straight shed, it also shows, behind the front end of the engine, the entrance to No.2 roundhouse which cut into the south wall of No.3 shed and the north-west corner of the straight shed. *M.Joyce per Gresley Society.*

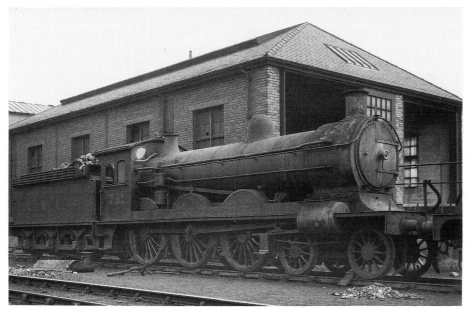

B13 No.751, alongside the elevated repair shop roads in August 1935. Looking extremely neglected and dirty, the Gateshead built 4-6-0 had been a long-time resident at Dairycoates and ended its days there when it was withdrawn nine months after this photograph was taken. Amongst other duties undertaken by this class of engine, the working of the various fish trains out of the city was probably their most important task, Dairycoates having fourteen of the fifty strong class for this work at Grouping. *Authors collection.*

9890, one of Botanic's A8 Class tank engines, waits to enter the repair shop at Dairycoates in April 1947 for attention. These large and capable 'Pacific tanks' were employed by Botanic Gardens on passenger trains to Leeds also to Bridlington and Scarborough. The A8's started life as NER Raven Class H1 4-4-4 tank engines, all 45 built at Darlington between 1913 and 1922. The LNER rebuilt the whole of the class into 4-6-2's during the mid 1930s, an act that prolonged their lives, for most survived to the late 1950's. *H.C.Casserley.*

An atmospheric view inside No.4 roundhouse circa 1955 with resident K3 No.61847 *(left)* and snowplough fitted J39 No.64914 ready for their next duties. Notice even then the turntable pit guard rails were somewhat the worse for wear and also the lack of smokejacks over the nearest two roads. *Authors collection.*

Probably No.3 roundhouse on Saturday 18th August 1952 with a selection of resident tank engines ranged around the turntable for the weekend respite. The five engines are of four different classes, J71, N10, N8 and J72. *R.K.Blencowe collection.*

A group of the former Western Region 0-6-0 diesel hydraulic locomotives stable around the outside turntable at Dairycoates on the 2nd March 1967. Some of them barely two years old on this date, they were prime candidates for sale to industrial concerns when BR had no more work for them and withdrew them virtually en masse by the end of the decade. The lone Class 08 shunter had a more successful and prolonged career as one of a class numbering over a thousand, spanning a working life of over 40 years and scattered to all parts of the country. *The Rev. David Benson.*

Three fitters going off-duty walk past D9503 and D9515 at Dairycoates at the end of the early shift on Thursday 2nd March 1967. *The Rev. David Benson*

THE ENGINE SHED AT SPRINGHEAD

The Hull & Barnsley Railway began operation in July 1885 with a stock of 42 engines, of which about 30 were based at the Hull end of the line. A shed on the Alexandra Dock catered for the engines which did the shunting there, but the 2-4-0 and 0-6-0 tender engines working the main line had a substantial shed provided for them at Springhead, some 3¼ miles west of the centre of Hull. It was a straight shed, with access at both ends, and after extensions were made to it in 1890, 1897, and 1906, it was about 380 feet long and 90 feet wide, with eight through roads. A water softening plant was installed as early as 1890; in 1906 the turntable was replaced by a new one 55 feet diameter to cope with the big 0-8-0 mineral engines then on order, and in July 1908 a new coaling stage was brought into use, but this shed never rated getting a mechanical coaler. Such then were the facilities which the Hull & Barnsley handed over to the North Eastern Railway when absorbed at the end of March 1922, and as I came to know them from 1931.

The final Hull & Barnsley engine was delivered new in December 1914, bringing their total to 186, all built by outside contractors. In 1917 they withdrew 0-6-0 No.17A and 2-4-0 No.38A, and in 1920 also scrapped three more 0-6-0's Nos 14A, 21A, and 31A, all five being original 1885 stock. So the North Eastern took over 181 engines, did not like what they saw of many of them, and condemned no less than 42 of them between April and December 1922. Coming under the heading of 'Hull's Railways', it is pertinent to mention that the engine portion of No.48, one of the Alexandra Dock 0-4-0 tanks,

was presented to the Hull Technical College in Park Street so that engineering students could examine its rather intricate valve gear. I remember seeing it when I attended in the 1931/2 winter, but it went for metal salvage early in the 1939 war. After the North Eastern's slaughter, they had to make replacements from their own stock, so of the 120 engines allocated to Springhead shed at the start of the LNER, 99 were Hull & Barnsley, and 21 were from the North Eastern. Changed traffic arrangements by the LNER management led to the H & B's five 4-4-0 passenger engines being moved in July 1924 to work from Botanic Gardens shed, the trains then using Paragon station, which enabled Cannon Street terminus and Beverley Road station to be closed. By the end of 1927 all the North Eastern engines had returned to their parent system, and Springhead's allocation had been reduced to only 74. Starting in September 1929, the coal trains from West Riding pits to Hull began to be hauled by 2-8-0 class 04 engines bought cheaply from the Government's Railway Operating Division and by 1931, Springhead was home to 22 of them, but they had displaced 14 H&B 0-6-0's and 13 of the big 0-8-0's, most of them going to be scrapped.

Trade conditions in the early 1930's meant less work still for Springhead's allocation which continued steadily downwards, and when the war began in 1939, it was no more than a quarter of the January 1923 total. Then in 1940, the 2-8-0's were sent to West Hartlepool to help work

coal traffic on the main line to London, because no longer could it be shipped down the East Coast because of mines, and enemy action by E-boats and submarines. In lieu of the mineral engines North Eastern Q6 class   0-8-0's were sent, but they too were needed for trains away from the coastal region so did not stay long, leaving Hull in the comprehensive March 1943 re-allocation throughout the whole of the N.E.Area. Surely Springhead's nadir was reached when they were regarded as worth only ten C6 class in exchange. Six of those Atlantics with four-coupled driving wheels as big as 6' 10" diameter, were almost 40 years old, and the other four were well over 30, so must have been considered to be 'expendable' when sent to an air raid prone danger zone. Two heavy raids in June and July 1943 caused further widespread damage and another 38 deaths in the city, but fortunately none to its engine sheds. Unable to find suitable work for express passenger engines it was not surprising that by October 1944 all had left, indeed some went straight to Darlington works for cut up.

After nationalisation, the run-down of the allocation spread to the shed building, and by 1955 all eight roads were roofless. Then four of the roads were re-habilitated to provide a temporary base for the new diesel multiple unit railcars, being drafted in to work the local passenger trains, until the complete re-building of Botanic Gardens shed was completed to house them. Springhead officially closed to steam on 15th December 1958, although all the remaining engines had transferred to Dairycoates on

Trying to out-do NER with their Dairycoates shed view of 1913, the H&B seem to have arranged a similar gathering at the west end of Springhead shed although without the white paint. More likely this was the usual Sunday scene at any period up to 1922. Taken from Locomotive Junction the photograph depicts from left to right; the coal stage; the locomotive works before the north side shop was extended to the same length as the shop nearest the engine shed which can be seen on the right. *J.G.Gregory.*

At a later date, probably 1919/20, wagons are more in evidence on the shed yard. Locomotives are represented by a couple of 0-6-0s and a handful on the works lines. *Authors collection.*

30th November. Maintenance and servicing of the diesel railcars and a handful of diesel shunters continued until July 1961 when Botanic Gardens took them over completely, leaving just an empty shell. Vandalism accelerated its fate, so it was totally demolished, the site was cleared and to-day, one cannot even determine just where the 8-road shed stood. As I write this, my wife is attending an Inner Wheel coffee morning in a member's house which stands on the sidings connected with the shed.

For more than fifty years, Springhead shed building showed one of those small quirky details that dedicated researchers find so interesting. One Saturday afternoon in May 1936 shedmaster George Gregory was showing me some of his photographs of the H & B big 0-8-0's and I asked why, on the first ten, the front sandbox fillers were outside the running plate but on the five later ones they were through the plate. He took me to the left-hand doorway at the west end of the shed and pointed to where a portion had been chipped away from the vertical edge at about 3' 6'' from ground level. One of the lines entering that doorway was on a slight curve, and when the big 0-8-0's arrived in 1907, their front overhang caused the filler cap to strike the wall. It was cheaper to chip the wall away slightly than to alter ten engines - and also gave a quicker remedy. The three months later delivery of the other five enabled their makers to be told to modify them. There is photographic evidence of both these ways of obtaining the required clearance. The first ten were never altered, and the chipped away wall remained so even thirty years after those engines were scrapped. Just one more addition to the store of useless knowledge, but fascinating to the cognoscenti.

W.D. Renumbering *see over*

In 1947/48 eighteen W.D. 2-8-0's were received 'on loan', but twelve were returned in 1948. The six which remained had W.D. 7xxxx numbers changed to B.R. 9xxxx series from March 1949 as follows: 77018/90116, 77104/90567, 77135/90586, 77175/90160, 77260/90217, 77320/90233. W.D. 79227, transferred from Dairycoates in 1950, was not renumbered to 90688 until October 1952.

(below) **The eastern end of the shed in early LNER days when H&B locos still had a presence.** *Authors collection.*

HULL SPRINGHEAD

Allocation as at 1st January 1923:-
D22 808, 1538
D24 2425, 2426, 2427, 2428, 2429
F8 262
J23 2433, 2435, 2441, 2442, 2443, 2444, 2445, 2446, 2447, 2453, 2454, 2455, 2457, 2458, 2459, 2460, 2470, 2471, 2472, 2473, 2474, 2475, 2476, 2477, 2513, 2514, 2515, 2516, 2517, 2518, 2519, 2520, 2521, 2522
J25 2047, 2051
J28 2406, 2408, 2409, 2411, 2412, 2413, 2416, 2417, 2418, 2420, 2421, 2422, 2423, 2424, 2538, 2539, 2540, 2541, 2542
J75 2492, 2493, 2495, 2523, 2524, 2528, 2529, 2530, 2531, 2532
J80 2448, 2449, 2450
N8 351
N9 1617, 1649, 1650, 1653
N11 2478, 2479, 2480, 2482
N12 2485
N13 2405, 2407, 2410, 2419, 2534, 2535, 2536, 2537
Q5 578, 656, 764, 1032
Q6 1249, 1280, 1311, 2230, 2237, 2277, 2299
Q10 2498, 2499, 2500, 2501, 2502, 2503, 2504, 2505, 2506, 2507, 2508, 2509, 2510, 2511, 2512

To avoid confusion, numbers used for exH&B engines are those allocated to them in February 1924.

Subsequent changes to the allocation up to closure in 1958 were as follows:

1923	IN	J27 938, 2386, 2388, 2389, 2391; Q6 2234, 2301 (7)
	OUT	J25 2047, 2051 (2)
1924	IN	J23 2430; J27 917; J78 590; Q5 443, 645, 785, 1002, 1110; Q6 1292, 2243, 2252, 2264 (12)
	OUT	D22 808, 1538; D24 2425, 2426, 2427, 2428, 2429; F8 262; J27 2386, 2389; J78 590; N12 2485; Q5 578, 764, 1032; Q6 1249, 1280, 2234, 2237, 2299; Q10 2500 (21)
1925	IN	A7 1136; Q5 652, 715, 1032; Q6 2231, 2247, 2294 (7)
	OUT	J75 2523, 2528, 2529, 2532; J80 2448; N8 351; N9 1653; Q5 443, 652, 656, 785; Q10 2508 (12)
1926	IN	(0)
	OUT	J23 2430, 2442, 2443; J27 917, 938, 2388; Q5 1110 (7)
1927	IN	N12 2491; Y1 79 (2)
	OUT	A7 1136; J23 2433, 2447, 2454, 2455, 2470, 2515, 2521, 2522; J27 2391; N9 1617, 1649, 1650; N11 2480, 2482; Q5 645, 715, 1002, 1032; Q6 1292, 1311, 2230, 2231, 2243, 2247, 2252, 2264, 2277, 2294, 2301; Q10 2501, 2502 (32)
1928	IN	Q10 2501, 2502 (2)
	OUT	J23 2435, 2477; J28 2408, 2416 (4)
1929	IN	O4 6577, 6578, 6579, 6580, 6581, 6584, 6609, 6610, 6612, 6613, 6614, 6615, 6618 (13)
	OUT	J23 2445, 2446, 2453, 2459, 2475, 2517; N11 2479; Q10 2499, 2501, 2504, 2505, 2506, 2507, 2509, 2510, 2511, 2512 (17)
1930	IN	N13 2533; O4 6261, 6262, 6583, 6607, 6608, 6616, 6617, 6630, 6631, 6632; Y1 187 (12)
	OUT	J23 2474, 2476, 2513, 2514; J28 2413, 2420; N11 2478; O4 6577, 6578; Q10 2503 (10)
1931	IN	J23 2469; N12 2486; O4 6611; Y3 117 (4)
	OUT	J23 2516, 2518; J80 2449, 2450; Q10 2498, 2502; Y1 79, 187 (8)
1932	IN	(0)
	OUT	J23 2458, 2471, 2472; Y3 117 (4)
1933	IN	J23 2452, 2461, 2464, 2465; N11 2482 (5)
	OUT	J23 2457, 2461, 2469, 2473; J28 2411, 2412, 2417, 2418, 2421, 2422, 2424, 2538, 2540, 2541; O4 6261, 6262, 6580, 6614, 6615 (19)
1934	IN	J21 564; J75 2525; N13 2415 (3)
	OUT	J21 564; J23 2441, 2444, 2452, 2460, 2464, 2465; J28 2423, 2539, 2542; O4 6579, 6611 (12)
1935	IN	J21 613, 1558; J25 25, 2038 (4)
	OUT	J23 2519, 2520; J25 25; J28 2406, 2409; O4 6632 (6)
1936	IN	(0)
	OUT	J21 1558; N12 2491 (2)
1937	IN	J21 1305; N12 2488 (2)
	OUT	J25 2038; N11 2482; J75 2492, 2493, 2495, 2524, 2525, 2530, 2531; N12 2486 (10)
1938	IN	O4 6615 (1)
	OUT	N12 2488 (1)
1939	IN	J21 1510; N11 2478, 2479, 2480 (4)
	OUT	J21 613 (1)
1940	IN	Q6 1284, 2217, 2220, 2227, 2229, 2234, 2239, 2244, 2254, 2257,

1940 IN cont		2264, 2283, 2291 (13)
	OUT	J21 1305; O4 6581, 6583, 6607, 6608, 6609, 6610, 6612, 6613, 6615, 6616, 6617, 6618, 6630, 6631 (15)
1941	IN	Q6 2275 (1)
	OUT	O4 6584 (1)
1942	IN	J21 1810; N12 2486 (2)
	OUT	N13 2407, 2537 (2)
1943	IN	C6 295, 649, 698, 699, 702, 703, 705, 742, 1753, 1776, 1794; J24 1892; J25 1723, 1976, 2056, 2139; N8 267, 348, 445, 1104; N11 2481, 2482; Q6 1276, 2219, 2241 (25)
	OUT	C6 649, 699, 703, 705, 1794; N11 2478; N13 2405, 2419, 2533, 2534, 2535, 2536; Q6 1284, 2217, 2220, 2227, 2229, 2234, 2239, 2244, 2254, 2257, 2264, 2275, 2283, 2291 (26)
1944	IN	(0)
	OUT	C6 295, 698, 702, 742, 1753, 1776; J24 1892; J25 1723; N11 2479, 2482; Q6 1276, 2219, 2241 (13)
1945	IN	A7 1136, 1174, 1190; J25 1723; O1 6334, 6350, 6578, 6630; O4 5008, 5404, 6211, 6352, 6501, 6581, 6606, 6615; Y8 559 (17)
	OUT	N8 267, 348, 445, 1104; N11 2481; O1 6350 (6)
1946	IN	N13 2405, 2407, 2534, 2537; O7 3001, 3012, 3030, 3045, 3113 (9)
	OUT	J21 1510; N11 2480; O1 6334, 6578, 6630; O4 5008, 5404, 6211, 6581, 6606 (10)
1947	IN	WD 77004, 77018, 77067, 77075, 77104, 77128, 77138, 77149, 77167, 77218, 77338, 77353 (12)
	OUT	J21 1810; O7 3001, 3012, 3030, 3045, 3113 (6)
1948	IN	O7 3007, 3008, 3009, 3010, 3011, 3047, 3052, 3057, 3094, 3108, 3149, 3176; WD 77135, 77175, 77260, 77320, 77468, 79280 (18)
	OUT	N12 2486; N13 2405; O7 3052; WD 77004, 77067, 77075, 77128, 77138, 77149, 77167, 77218, 77338, 77353, 77468, 79280 (15)
1949	IN	A7 9789; J21 5112; J25 5667, 5705; O4 3754; WD 90382, 90677 (7)
	OUT	J21 5112; J25 1976, 2056, 2139; N13 2407; O4 6615; O7 3008, 3009, 3011, 3057; WD 90382, 90677 (12)
1950	IN	N13 9111; O1 3712, 3740, 3760, 3856, 3874; O7 3011, 3157; WD 90571, 90586, 90661, 90677, 90688 (14)
	OUT	O1 3712, 3740, 3760, 3856, 3874; O4 3754, 6352, 6501; O7 3007, 3047; WD 90160, 90217, 90378, 90567, 90586 (15)
1951	IN	A7 9780, 9784; O7 3146, 90427; WD 90233, 90663, 90704 (7)
	OUT	A7 9789; J25 1723, 5667, 5705; O7 3010, 3052; WD 90233, 90704 (8)
1952	IN	A7 9783; O7 3082; WD 90623 (3)
	OUT	N13 2410, 2415, 9111 (3)
1953	IN	A7 9787; J71 8284; N8 9378; O7 90511 (4)
	OUT	N13 2534, 2537 (2)
1954	IN	A7 9771, 9778; J72 8743, 8746; O7 3061 (5)
	OUT	A7 1136, 1174, 9771, 9780, 9787; J71 8284; J72 8743 (7)
1955	IN	A7 9772; WD 90352 (2)
	OUT	A7 9778, 1190; N8 9378; O7 3082, 3146; WD 90663 (6)
1956	IN	A7 9782, 9786; J25 5677; J73 8361; O7 90482; WD 90378; DES 13232, 13233 (8)
	OUT	A7 9783, 9784; J25 5677; J72 8746 (4)
1957	IN	J25 5663, 5685; O7 90503; BR3 77000 (4)
	OUT	A7 9772, 9782, 9786; O7 3108, 3149, 3176 (6)
1958	IN	J73 8360; BR3 77010; LM2 46409 (3)
	OUT	J25 5663, 5685; J73 8360, 8361; O7 3011, 3061, 3094 3106, 3157, 3182, 90482, 90511; WD 90116, 90233, 90352, 90378, 90571, 90586, 90623, 90661, 90677, 90688; DES 13232, 13233; BR3 77000, 77010; LM2 46409 (27)

Closure.

Springhead shed was officially closed to steam locomotives on 15th December 1958, although all 27 on its final allocation had been transferred away on 30th November. It continued to maintain diesel locomotives and railcars until July 1961 when that activity ceased. The buildings were demolished and the site was then cleared completely.

In 1929 thirteen Class O4 2-8-0's arrived at Springhead to begin a relationship with that shed which lasted until 1950. In a bid to rid the LNER of the non-standard H&B Class Q10 engines, the authorities sent more of the former R.O.D. locomotives to Springhead the following year. This view shows the Shedmaster J.G.Gregory (second from lelf) posing with the first of the new arrivals, 6581, in September 1929. *Authors collection.*

The shed and works complex at Springhead became somewhat, but not quite, surplus to requirements, and stored locomotives could be found on the redundant sidings around the works and shed area from the late 1920s onwards. H&B locomotives were among the first to be stored in any number and over the ensuing years the types became many and varied. Here eight J75's form a line at the east end of the shed in 1937, after withdrawal and awaiting the call to Darlington for scrapping.*Authors coll.*

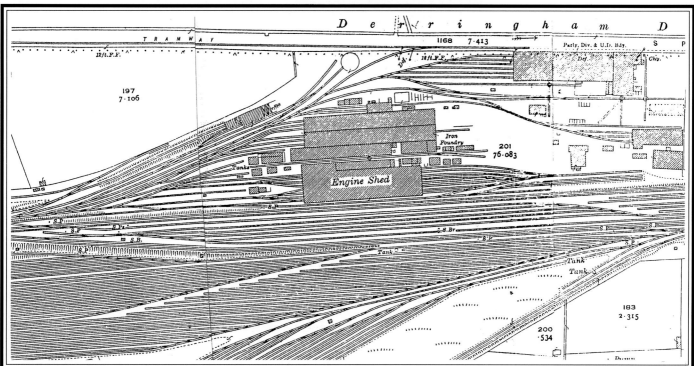

Springhead Engine Shed and Works 1928. *Crown copyright reserved.*

In the final years of its life Springhead shed was partly adapted to cater for the needs of the local d.m.u. fleet, one of which is just visible in the left background. Prominent in this picture of 1st June 1958, is former LMS Ivatt 2-6-0 No.46409 of 1946 vintage. This was the only engine of its class allocated to Hull, and even then it was only resident for a short period between May and September 1958. Chalked on the smoke box door is the pilot or trip number 'S2', this was an early morning pilot and commenced with the driver signing on duty at 4.50 a.m. It worked to Ella Street and Sculcoates followed by a trip to Albert Dock, and then light engine back to shed. The other two engines in this view, both WD 2-8-0s, are more familiar to local eyes. Stood on the right is 90661, but a positive identification of the rear engine is difficult. The shed was by now roofless, and within less than six months would lose its allocation. *Mike Lake*.

By the early 1960s as far as local passenger trains were concerned the changeover to diesel traction was almost complete. Many of the surviving steam engines were put into store either pending disposal or seasonal fluctuations in traffic. Here at Springhead shed are four members of LNER class D49, but only two can be positively identified, 62740 THE BEDALE nearest the camera, and 62727 THE QUORN standing beneath the re-roofed section of the shed. Unfortunately the picture is undated so I cannot say with any certainty if any of the engines ever steamed again. The nearer two have their chimneys covered over, a sure sign they are in store and out of traffic. *Neville Stead.*

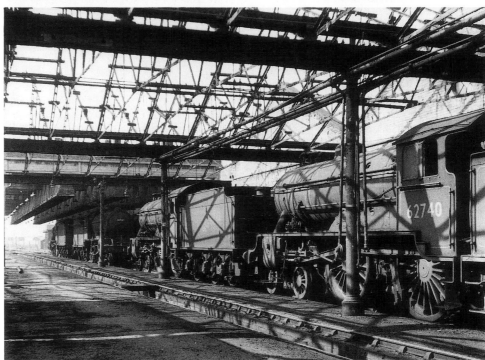

The demolition gang has moved onto the Springhead site. This undated view, looking east, shows the remains of the engine shed strewn around the floor. On the right, concrete columns which were erected for the re-roofing of the mid 50's, stand as a final reminder that an engine shed once stood here. To the left the former locomotive works was to suffer the same fate as the shed; its site now houses people and not engines. *Authors collection.*

THE ENGINE SHED AT ALEXANDRA DOCK

The dock itself was opened on July 16th 1885, and goods traffic on the railway began four days later. For the considerable amount of wagon movement on the lines around the dock the Hull & Barnsley provided twelve 0-6-0 tank engines numbered 1 to 12, which were available for the start of traffic. To them, in 1886-89 they added six smaller 0-4-0 tank engines numbered 43 to 48, which were better able to cope with the sharp curves on many of the dock lines. Those eighteen spent practically the whole of their lives (all were withdrawn from service in 1922) on the dock estate, travelling no further afield than the 5½ miles to, and from, the Company's workshops at Springhead for servicing and repairs. To give them some shelter, the home for them on the dock was a shed built of wood which spanned two parallel lines, each having an inspection pit below rail level. The covered accommodation had a length of 95 feet, making 190 feet available under cover, but the eighteen engines placed buffer to buffer totalled a length of 470 feet, so it was clearly intended that at least half of them would have to cope with inclement weather as best they could when they were not working. That wood structure was never extended, or improved, and by 1913 was reported as beyond repair, and needing to be replaced. The 1914-18 war prevented anything

being done; even if the intention was there, the money for it was not forthcoming. Quite soon after the war it became apparent that the Hull & Barnsley Railway was coming to the end of its independent existence, so there was no profit from spending money for someone else to benefit thereby. The wood building must have been soundly constructed in the 1880's because despite its dilapidation, it continued to be used until December 1927 when, helped by some wintry winds, it just *had* to be demolished. An LNER Traffic Committee meeting on the 30th July 1925 recommended closure of the shed at an estimated cost of £2,432 for demolition which in turn would bring estimated annual savings of £2,500. No replacement was ever provided; the two roads with their inspection pits continued to be occupied at weekends by a double line of engines, just as before. The meagre office facilities required were catered for in a time-served passenger vehicle parked on an adjoining siding. Neither the 1939-45 war, nor nationalisation made the slightest difference, and Alexandra Dock still had its own 'shed' allocation until October 27th 1963, when its 14 remaining locos (by then all diesels) were transferred to Dairycoates shed. That transfer was only effective at weekends, because a signing-on point was maintained at the dock, and

engines still stood there in the open when not in service, until the dock itself was closed in 1982. Throughout the almost 100 years were tank engines used on the dock, so no turntable was provided at the shed, nor did it ever have a coaling stage. Improved trading, and labour conditions enabled Alexandra Dock to be reopened at an official ceremony on 16th July 1991, the 106th anniversary of its original opening, but, sadly by then all rail access to the dock had been removed completely.

Tender engines did work to the western end of the dock, where for some years there was a small passenger station used solely by emigrants from Europe to the United States of America, who arrived in the dock by ship, and were then taken by train to Liverpool to join another ship to continue their journey. Adjacent to that station there was a turntable 50 feet in diameter which the 2-4-0 engines used for those trains could turn on. By 1897 emigrant traffic through Alexandra Dock had dwindled, ceasing altogether by 1906, when, it was concentrated on the North Eastern's provision for it through Albert Dock. For a time in 1919, the station was used for passenger traffic in the other direction, namely the repatriation of German prisoners-of-war, and the 2-4-0 engines were still available to do the dock working again.

Alexandra Dock engine shed circa 1925 with the slateless roof offering little if any shelter from the elements. Five of the tiny Y7 0-4-0 tanks are in evidence along with Class J74 0-6-0T. The tall chimney in the background belongs to the Alexandra Dock hydraulic engine house. *Authors coll.*

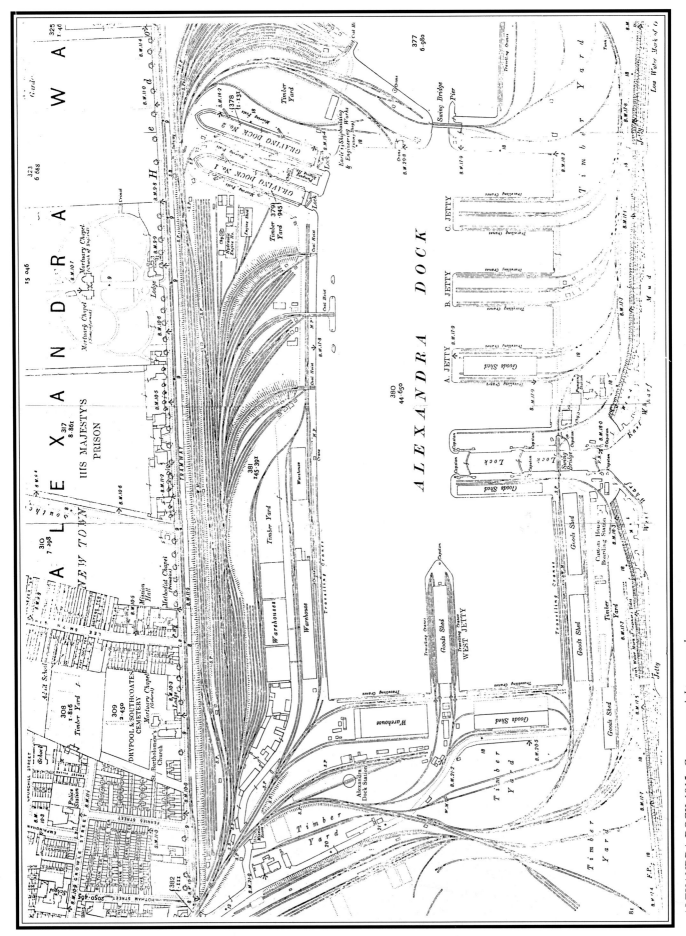

ALEXANDRA DOCK 1915. *Crown copyright reserved.*

HULL ALEXANDRA DOCK

Allocation as at 1st January 1923:-
J71 225, 239, 286, 347, 451, 493, 499
J74 20, 64, 82, 88, 461, 467, 489, 662
J75 3113, 3115, 3116 (renumbered 2494, 2496, 2497 in 1924)
J76 171
Y7 24, 900, 1302, 1798, 1799
From April 1922 the four NER types had replaced 12 G1 and 6 K H&B classes.
Subsequent changes to the allocation during the next forty years were as follows:

1923	IN	Y7 984, 985 (2)
	OUT	(0)
1924	IN	(0)
	OUT	J71 347, 499 (2)
1925	IN	J72 576, 1744, 2308 (3)
	OUT	J71 451 (1)
1926	IN	(0)
	OUT	J76 171 (1)
1927	IN	(0)
	OUT	(0)
1928	IN	(0)
	OUT	(0)
1929	IN	(0)
	OUT	(0)
1930	IN	(0)
	OUT	J74 64; Y7 1302 (2)
1931	IN	J71 27, 452 (2)
	OUT	J74 20, 82, 88, 461, 467, 489, 662; Y7 24, 900 (9)
1932	IN	(0)
	OUT	Y7 1798 (1)
1933	IN	J71 496 (1)
	OUT	J71 27 (1)
1934	IN	J75 2526, 2527 (2)
	OUT	(0)
1935	IN	(0)
	OUT	Y7 1799 (1)
1936	IN	(0)
	OUT	(0)
1937	IN	J71 449, 1083, 1084, 1199, 1864; J72 516, 1721, 1742; J73 546, 549, 550, 551, 552; J77 145, 199, 614, 948, 1340, 1341, 1433 (20)
	OUT	J71 225, 496; J75 2494, 2496, 2497, 2526, 2527 (7)
1938	IN	(0)
	OUT	J73 552 (1)
1939	IN	J72 462, 524, 571, 574, 1715, 2317, 2318; J73 545; J77 623, 1461 (10)
	OUT	J71 239, 286, 449, 452, 493, 1083, 1084, 1199, 1864; J72 2318; J77 623; Y7 984, 985 (13)
1940	IN	(0)
	OUT	J72 2308; J73 545, 546, 551 (4)
1941	IN	(0)
	OUT	J72 1715 (1)

1942	IN	(0)
	OUT	J72 1721, 1744; J77 1341 (3)
1943	IN	(0)
	OUT	(0)
1944	IN	(0)
	OUT	(0)
1945	IN	(0)
	OUT	(0)
1946	IN	J77 8402 (1) *
	OUT	J77 8419 (1)
1947	IN	(0)
	OUT	(0)
1948	IN	J77 8401, 8440 (2)
	OUT	J77 8390, 8395, 8406 (3)
1949	IN	J72 8676, 8743, 8746, 69001, 69002, 69003, 69009; N13 9111 (8)
	OUT	J72 8748; J77 8401 (2)
1950	IN	(0)
	OUT	N13 9111 (1)
1951	IN	(0)
	OUT	J77 8440 (1)
1952	IN	(0)
	OUT	J72 69002 (1)
1953	IN	J72 8741, 69010, 69011; DES 12113, 12114, 12115 (6)
	OUT	J72 8724, 8743, 8747; J77 8402, 8413 (5)
1954	IN	J72 8743, 8745, 8747; DES 12116, 12117, 12118, 12119, 12120 (8)
	OUT	(0)
1955	IN	DES 12121, 12122, 13139, 13140, 13141 (5)
	OUT	J72 69010 (1)
1956	IN	J72 8746; DES 13234, 13235, 13236 (4)
	OUT	J73 8361; DES 13139, 13140, 13141 (4)
1957	IN	J72 8672, 8741 (2)
	OUT	J72 8746, 8752 (2)
1958	IN	(0)
	OUT	J73 8360 (1)
1959	IN	(0)
	OUT	J72 8672, 8741 (2)
1960	IN	DM D2100, D2101, D2102, D2155, D2156, D2157 (6)
	OUT	J72 8676, 8745, 69003, 69009, 69010, 69011 (6)
1961	IN	(0)
	OUT	(0)
1962	IN	(0)
	OUT	DES 12122, D3234, D3235, D3236; DM D2100 (5)
1963	IN	(0)
	OUT	DES 12113, 12114, 12115, 12116, 12117, 12118, 12119, 12120, 12121; DM D2101, D2102, D2155, D2156, D2157 (14) **

* The eight J72, two J73 and seven J77 were renumbered.
** All fourteen locomotives were transferred to Dairycoates on 27th October 1963 and Alexandra Dock then ceased to have any locomotives allocated to it.

J71 No.1083 joined the Alexandra Dock complement in 1937 along with four other members of the class. This NER design of 1886 had been associated with Alexandra Dock since 1922 when seven of them, as NER Class E, replaced a similar number of Hull & Barnsley engines. In 1939 all nine J71's still allocated to the dockside shed were sent away, displaced by another NER design the J72. Not all the J71's went to the scrap heap though, of the nine only No.493 was scrapped in July 1939 whilst the others went on working into BR days, some into the early 1960's. 1083, here on the shed yard in September 1938, returned to Dairycoates in June 1939 from where it worked until it was withdrawn in April 1957 as 68252.
Authors collection.

NER Class H 0-4-0T (later LNER Class Y7) no.24 outside Alexandra Dock engine shed circa 1925. The initials N.E. on the side tank came about when new plating was welded over the letter R. at the cab end of the tank so foreshadowing an event of 1943 when N E only was applied in place of the usual L N E R due to wartime ecenomy measures. During 1929-31 nine were sold to industrial concerns, and in 1931/2 seven were scrapped out of the 24 of the class. By then, only three remained at the Dock; 1799 went to Tyne Dock in 1935 and 984/5 left Hull in October 1939. *Real Photos.*

The ramshackle wooden engine shed shortly before it was demolished in 1928. The inward lean of the south wall can be clearly seen and propping up the lintel over the entrance is a temporary stanchion of un-planed timber. Inside the shed J75 No.2495, from Springhead, receives some minor repair. *Authors collection.*

The locomotive class changes and additions at Alexandra Dock in 1937 also brought another new class to the shed when beside the seven J77's, five J73's (half of the class) arrived. In April 1949 wearing its LNER 1946 number (previous number was 550), 8361 stands on the coaling stage road at the shed. The other locomotives in view are stabled on the roads once covered by the engine shed and already some of them are showing evidence of new ownership. 8361 was the last J73 to leave Alexandra Dock, as 68361 in 1956. In the right background two ships can be seen on the stocks of Nos. 1 and 2 Graving Docks.

Authors collection.

THE SHED KNOWN AS BOTANIC GARDENS

The need for the building of a complete new shed, on a 'green field' site which arose here in 1900 took place at just the right time to be a boon to Hull's locomotive power. The North Eastern Railway required to enlarge Paragon station considerably, and could only do so on its north side. That involved removal of the three-road shed which had been erected as part of the 1848 station, and also of the later shed built at its north-west corner. Both those sheds had been laid out on the basis of housing engines of the 2-4-0 type, of which Fletcher's 901 and 1440 classes had 37ft. 1in. total wheelbase, and an overall length of 48ft. 6ins. Even the 'Tennant' class (which became E5 on the LNER) only exceeded those lengths by 18 inches.

Around 1900 however, the NER Locomotive Superintendent was busy re-stocking the sheds on the East Coast main line with 4-4-0 and 4-6-0 types (known to us as D20 and B13) which were much more powerful, and which then released the smaller 4-4-0's hitherto used, to be cascaded to areas such as Hull where train loads were more limited, and the terrain pro-vided easy gradients. Those 4-4-0's (which the LNER classed as D17, D22 and D23) were all about 8 feet longer than the 2-4-0 classes, and the timing was right for a new shed to accommodate them, with stalls, and turntables of appropriate length. It would have been costly otherwise to modify Paragon turntable and the shed to take them, and we could well have been left to use the existing stock of 2-4-0's as best we could, maybe up to, and possibly through World War One. So the new shed at Botanic Gardens opened in 1901 although preparations for it had begun in 1898 when the lines leading to it were laid in, and passed Board of Trade inspection. It was almost entirely concerned with passenger train services, and normally its allocation did not work further afield than Sheffield (Victoria) via Doncaster, Leeds, Scarborough, York, and the branches to Hornsea and Withernsea. Two turntables, each of 50 ft diameter, with 24 radiating stalls were provided, and could usually house the full allocation under cover. Significant changes were the influx of Sentinel railcars in 1929, and from 1932, the arrival of the much more powerful 4-4-0's of the Shire and Hunt D49 classes. For them, a new coaling plant of the labour-saving type was erected. Post 1939-45 war a modest number of Thompson B1 class 4-6-0's came to take over the heavier duties, mainly those to Doncaster, and to Leeds, and then in the mid 1950's "modernisation" struck.

During 1956/57 a complete new building replaced that of 1901, over the existing turntable and stalls of No.2 shed, whilst what had been No.1 shed had its turntable taken out and radiating pits filled in. During the following two years the turntable of No.2 shed was taken out and the pits and stalls filled in. The whole shed was then converted from the roundhouse type to a straight one to house diesel mechanical railcar multiple units for which it was re-opened officially on 13th June 1959, its remaining steam locomotives all having been transferred to Dairycoates shed. It continued to service and refuel diesel trains, cars, and shunting locomotives until they dwindled steadily, and from January 1987 we have not had a single locomotive allocated to any Hull shed although d.m.u's are still serviced and refueled.

Botanic Gardens shed yard in May 1952, virtually unchanged from the day the depot opened in 1901. An unidentified but fairly clean B1 stands near to the roundhouse entrance. On the far left is the old coaling stage, long superseded by the mechanical coaling plant, erected in 1932 and just out of picture behind the tall water tower. Although locomotives were served by the mechanical coaler, the old stage continued in use for the Sentinel railcars. The outside turntable was put down shortly after the shed opened and was used by 'foreign' engines to enable a fast turn-round for working back home same day. The ubiquitous push-bikes are in evidence and the eagle-eyed will notice fireman Ernie Wyvill's 'tandem' propped against the office block end wall. Although not opened for use until 1901, the connections from the shed yard to the main lines were laid down by October 1898, the Board of Trade inspecting the relevant works during that month. *R.K.Blencowe collection.*

A dismal Botanic Gardens in November 1955 looking north across the No.2 turntable. The centre section of the roof has been taken down in preparation for the massive rebuilding. Locomotives around the turntable are from left; A8 69879, B1 61068, G5 67253, L1 67765 and D49 62737. Outside a G5 acts as shed pilot. *Authors collection.*

A view across the No.1 turntable towards No.2. No engines are stabled in this portion of the shed as contractors work to strip away the old fabric of the building. The coaling plant stands above the gloom untouched by the modernisation scheme. *British Railways.*

By early 1958 the centre section of the roof over No.2 turntable had been replaced with a modular concrete structure resting on steel beams, the outside smaller sections of the original roof were, it will be noticed, still in situ, with temporary sections bridging the gap between old and new. Steam locomotives continued to use this part of the shed until they were evicted so that the turntable could be taken out and further work could be undertaken. No.1 shed had in the meantime been converted into a straight shed, or at least the floor layout had, ready for maintaining the forthcoming diesel railcar fleet. Although the partition wall and roof have yet to be added the concrete pits are apparent in this view. *Authors collection.*

(below) The view from the north end of No.2 shed in January 1959 after the steam locos had been ejected to the yard and the remaining turntable had been removed and the pit filled in. The area once occupied by the turntable now taken up by two continuous concrete pits. No.1 shed roof is somewhat different from that of No.2, there being no need for a high lofty span covering any turntable. The precast concrete beams employed are to a design first used by the LMS in 1937 and subsequently adopted by the North Eastern Region, amongst others, for rebuilding straight road engine sheds. The running rails of the new diesel depot were placed onto the stanchions projecting from the sub floor, enabling fitters to have a greater and more accessible working area whilst maintaining the diesels. Botanic Gardens re-opened for its new role less than six months later. *British Railways.*

HULL BOTANIC GARDENS

Locomotive allocation as at 1st January 1923:-

D17/1 1620, 1622, 1623, 1626, 1628, 1629, 1630, 1633, 1635, 1639.
D19   1619.
D20   712, 1234, 2014, 2102, 2103.
D22   42, 85, 96, 194, 340, 777, 803, 1137, 1534, 1540, 1543.
D23   23, 222, 223, 258, 337, 521, 557, 675, 676, 677, 679.
F8   187, 1322, 1582.
G5   435, 436, 1334, 1703.
G6   247, 341.
X2   957.

Subsequent changes to the allocation up to 1959 were as follows:

1923	IN	(0)
	OUT	(0)
1924	IN	B14 2111, 2112, 2113, 2114, 2115; D20 1026; D23 1107; D24 2425, 2426, 2427, 2428, 2429; J72 462 (13)
	OUT	D23 679 (1)
1925	IN	D17/1 1634, 1638; D21 1239, 1245, 1246; D22 115, 117, 230, 514, 1532, 1536, 1539; D23 1120; G6 358 (14)
	OUT	B14 2111, 2112, 2113, 2114, 2115; D17/1 1622, 1628, 1629, 1630, 1635, 1638, 1639; D20 712; D22 42, 1534; D23 23, 222, 223, 258, 337, 675, 676 (22)
1926	IN	D21 1240 (1)
	OUT	D19 1619; D20 1026 (2)
1927	IN	D17/2 1909, 1910; D20 1051; D22 777, 1540; G6 605 (6)
	OUT	D22 96, 777, 1540; D23 521; G6 247, 605 (6)
1928	IN	D20 2088; G5 1691, 1701, 2008; G6 60, 466, 1055 (7)
	OUT	D23 557, 1107; F8 187; G6 60, 341, 358, 1055 (7)
1929	IN	D20 2016, 2024; D22 356, 663, 1546; G5 2084, 2098; J77 623; Y1 19, 108 (10)
	OUT	D22 117, 514, 803, 1137, 1540; D23 677, 1120; G6 466; J72 462 (9)
1930	IN	C12 4514, 4541, 4545, 4550; D17/2 1922 (5)
	OUT	D22 194, 230, 777, 1532, 1539; F8 1582 (6)
1931	IN	B16 848, 849; C12 4542, 4543, 4546, 4547, 4549; D20 1026, 2109; K3 1108, 1119; X3 190 (12)
	OUT	D21 1239, 1240, 1245, 1246; D22 115, 1536; D24 2425, 2427; G5 435, 1334, 1703; K3 1108, 1119; X2 957 (14)
1932	IN	C12 4544; D17/1 1632; D49 253, 318, 320, 322, 327, 335; X2 957 (9)
	OUT	B16 848, 849; D17/1 1623, 1626; D17/2 1909, 1922; D22 85, 356, 663, 1543; F8 1322; X3 190 (12)
1933	IN	D3 4301, 4313, 4341, 4345, 4346; D49 282, 292 (7)
	OUT	D17/1 1620; D22 340; D24 2426, 2428; D49 253 (5)
1934	IN	C12 4519, 4524, 4534; D3 4350; D16/3 8817; D20 2026, 2101; D49 205, 214, 222 (10)
	OUT	D3 4301, 4341, 4345, 4346; D16/3 8817; D17/1 1632, 1633; D20 2017, 2024; D24 2429; G5 436, 1691, 1701, 2084, 2088, 2098 (16)
1935	IN	A6 694; A8 1520; D3 4074, 4075, 4080, 4304, 4349; D17/2 1871, 1873, 1905, 1907, 1909; D20 2024; D49 230, 238, 283, 318, 377 (18)
	OUT	A6 694; D3 4074, 4080, 4304, 4313; D17/1 1634; D17/2 1909, 1910; D20 2101; D22 1546; D49 222, 318, 320, 335 (14)
1936	IN	A8 1517, 2159, 2160; D3 4077, 4354; D49 220, 256 (7)
	OUT	D20 1026 (1)
1937	IN	D2 4180, 4386, 4398; D17/2 1874; G5 1691, 1703 (6)
	OUT	C12 4519, 4524, 4534; D3 4075, 4077, 4349, 4350, 4354; X2 957 (9)
1938	IN	A8 2160; D49 269, 336; G5 387, 1882, 2088, 2091 (7)
	OUT	A8 2160; C12 4550; D17/2 1874, 1905, 1907; D49 269, 318; G5 387 (8)
1939	IN	D2 4387; D17/1 1629; D17/2 1905; D49 234, 236, 245, 251, 253, 318, 320, 335; G5 441; J72 2317 (13)
	OUT	A8 1517; D2 4386; D20 1234, 2016; D49 205, 230, 282, 283, 292, 377; G5 1882; J72 2317; J77 623 (13)
1940	IN	A8 2151; D2 4398; D20 2103, 2110; G5 441, 2091 (6)
	OUT	D2 4398; D17/1 1629; D17/2 1905; D20 2014, 2101, 2103, 2109; G5 441, 2091 (9)
1941	IN	A8 1521; G5 1755 (2)
	OUT	D17/2 1871, 1873; D49 220; G5 1755; Y1 108 (5)
1942	IN	A8 2148, 2153; D20 2108, 2109; G5 387, 1740, 1884, 2082; Y1 187 (9)
	OUT	D49 251, 318, 336; G5 2091; Y1 19 (5)
1943	IN	D49 251, 318; G5 1737 (3)
	OUT	D49 253, 320 (2)
1944	IN	(0)
	OUT	D20 2109; G5 1737 (2)
1945	IN	D49 222, 273, 336; G5 1755 (4)
	OUT	D49 214; G5 441 (2)
1946	IN	A8 2147, 2161; B1 1010, 1071, 1074, 1080, 1084; D20 1665, 2013, 2018; D49 211, 247, 269, 364; G5 1693, 2083, 2092 (17)
	OUT	A8 2151, 2153; D20 1665, 2013, 2018 (5)

1947	IN	A6 9795, 9796; B1 1215; G5 7266, 7279 (5)
	OUT	A8 2161; C12 4546; D2 4180, 4387, 4398; D20 2103; G5 2083, 2088 (8)
1948	IN	A8 9877, 9879; B1 61304, 61305, 61306; D20 2372, 2379, 2387; L1 67719, 67721, 67727, 67728, 67730, 67736 (14)
	OUT	A8 1520, 1521, 2147, 2159; B1 1071, 1074, 1080, 1084; C12 4549; D20 1051, 2026, 2102, 2108, 2110; D49 273, 336; G5 1691, 7266, 7279 (19)
1949	IN	D20 2359, 2365, 2383, 2396; G5 7254; L1 67755, 67759, 67763, 67764, 67765 (10)
	OUT	A8 9867, 9879; D20 2359, 2365, 2372, 2379, 2387; D49 236, 251; G5 1755; L1 67721, 67727, 67728, 67730, 67736 (15)
1950	IN	A8 9854, 9859, 9866, 9873, 9876, 9878, 9880; C12 7354; D20 2345; L1 67755, 67759, 67763, 67764, 67766, 67766 (16)
	OUT	A6 9795; A8 9854, 9859, 9866, 9873, 9876, 9877, 9878, 9880; D49 256; L1 67719, 67755, 67759, 67763, 67764, 67765, 67766 (17)
1951	IN	A5 9802, 9811; A6 9791, 9793; D49 2717; G5 7253, 7337 (7)
	OUT	A6 9791, 9793; A8 2148; D20 2345, 2383, 2396; D49 269; Y1 187 (8)
1952	IN	A5 9836, 9837 (2)
	OUT	(0)
1953	IN	C12 7352, 7353; G5 7273 (3)
	OUT	A6 9796; C12 4543, 7354 (3)
1954	IN	A5 9835; B1 1068; G5 7261; L1 67754; LM3MT 40012, 40056, 40057, 40059, 40060, 40061 (10)
	OUT	D49 245; G5 387 (2)
1955	IN	A8 9860, 9867, 9879, 9881, 9886, 9888; D49 2701, 2707, 2710, 2750, 2766; L1 67755, 67764; BR3 77000, 77001, 77010; LM3MT 40017, 40045 (18)
	OUT	A8 9867; C12 4514, 4541, 4542, 4544, 4545, 4547, 7352, 7353; D49 2701, 2707, 2750, 2766; G5 1693, 2092, 7254, 7273; L1 67755, 67764 (19)
1956	IN	A8 9858, 9882; D20 2381, 2396; D49 2707, 2766; V1/V3 7638, 7663, 7677, 7685, 7686 (11)
	OUT	A8 9881; D49 234, 2707; G5 1703, 2082, 7337; L1 67754, 67755, 67759, 67763, 67764, 67765, 67766; LM3MT 40012, 40017, 40045, 40056, 40057, 40059, 40060, 40061 (21)
1957	IN	A5 9832; B1 1080, 1289; D49 2700, 2701, 2703, 2707, 2750; G5 7263, 7274, 7341; J71 8251; V3 7684 (13)
	OUT	A5 9835; A8 9858, 9860, 9882; D20 2381, 2396; D49 238, 335; G5 1740, 1884, 7253, 7261, 7341; J71 8251; V3 7685; BR3 77000 (16)
1958	IN	D49 2760; G5 7280, 7341; J73 8360; V1 7640; BR3 77000, 77010 (7)
	OUT	A5 9811, 9832, 9836, 9837; A8 9879, 9886, 9888; D49 2700, 2703, 211, 247, 2750, 222, 2766, 364; G5 7263, 7274, 7280, 7341; J73 8360; BR3 77010 (21)
1959	IN	V1/V3 7635, 7682 (2)
	OUT	A5 9802; B1 1010, 1068, 1080, 1215, 1289, 61304, 61305, 61306; D49 2701, 2707, 2710, 2717, 318, 322, 327, 2760; V1/V3 7635, 7638, 7640, 7663, 7677, 7682, 7684, 7686; BR3 77000, 77001, 77010 (28)

Note: Numbers in brackets indicate total movements for that year.

Botanic Gardens closed to steam locomotives on Sunday 14th June 1959, and that day all its 28 locomotives left, 25 going to Dairycoates shed, the other 3 (B1's 61068, 61304 and 61305) being transferred to Scarborough.

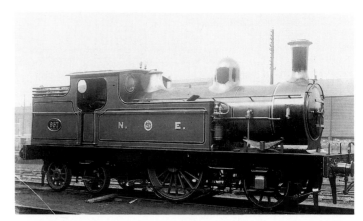

One of Botanic's more unusual members of its loco fleet was X2 class 2-2-4T no.957, a former NER BTP Class 0-4-4T from 1874 and rebuilt for 'special duties' in 1903. The duties entailed the locomotive hauling the inspection saloon of the Hull District Superintendent. From its rebuilding date until withdrawal in April 1937 this engine spent all of its working life at Botanic except for a six-month period over the winter of 1931/32, when it did a straight exchange with York's class X3 no.190. *LCGB coll.*

Railcars allocated to Botanic Gardens 1927-46

The railcars allocated to Botanic Gardens were numbered in the coaching stock series and thus duplicated locomotive stock numbers. In three cases, Botanic shed housed both railcar and D49 Class locomotive numbered 238, 273 and 283 simultaneously. Because the railcars were better known by name than by their number, a list of names is appended below the allocation list.

Year End D.E.*	Sentinel 2-Cyl	Sentinel 6-Cyl	A.W.
1927	21 (1)	(0)	(0)	
1928	26, 29, 210, 212, 273, 283 (7)	(0)	(0)	
1929	238, 244 (9)	2238, 2242, 2245 (3)	(0)	
1930	(9)	(3)	(0)	
1931	(9)	-2245 (2)	(0)	
1932	(9)	(2)	(0)	
1933	255, -273 (9)	(2)	(0)	
1934	22, -244 (9)	-2238 (1)	224 (1)	
1935	263, 265 (11)	(1)	(1)	
1936	267, -265, -283 (10)	(1)	232 (2)	
1937	(10)	(1)	(2)	
1938	-255 (9)	(1)	(2)	
1939	(9)	(1)	-224, -232 (0)	
1940	-22, -29, -263, -267 (5)	-2242 (0)	(0)	
1941	22, 273 (7)	(0)	(0)	
1942	-22 (6)	(0)	(0)	
1943	283, -212 (6)	(0)	(0)	
1944	253, 254, 263, 272, -21, -283 (8)	2267 (1)	(0)	
1945	-26, -210, -238 (5)	-2267 (0)	(0)	
1946	-253, -254, -263, -272, -273 (0)	(0)	(0)	

Notes:
1. Numbers prefixed by a minus sign indicate those railcars leaving the allocation that year.
2. Numbers in brackets indicate total allocation of that type in that year.
* Armstrong-Whitworth diesel electric.

Railcar names

Sentinel 2-Cylinder:-
 21 VALLIANT
 22 BRILLIANT
 26 TALLY-HO
 29 ROCKINGHAM
210 HIGHFLYER
212 ECLIPSE
238 YORKSHIRE HUZZAR
244 TRUE BRITON
253 RED ROVER
254 PHOENIX
255 PERSEVERANCE
263 NORTH STAR
265 NEPTUNE
267 LIBERTY
272 HERO
273 TRAFALGAR
283 TEAZLE

Sentinel 6-Cylinder:-
2238 CELERITY
2242 CORNWALLIS
2245 CRITERION
2267 RECOVERY

Armstrong-Whitworth D.E:-
224 LADY HAMILTON
232 NORTHUMBRIAN

Botanic Gardens diesel shunters 1970-87

On 21st September 1970, Dairycoates shed was closed and the remaining 24 diesel shunters (five Class 03 and nineteen Class 08) moved to Botanic Gardens shed, which then re-opened as a locomotive shed to maintain them, in addition to the railcars which it had been servicing since Springhead transferred them to Botanic on 30th November 1958.

When Goole shed was closed 4th February 1973, its allocation of five Class 03 diesel shunters were transferred to Botanic Gardens for maintenance. Through the 1970s industrial disputes involving dockers led to a progressive down-turn in traffic through the docks, culminating in the 1982 closure of Hull's second largest, Alexandra Dock. That run-down was mirrored by the decrease in the number of diesel shunters allocated to Botanic Gardens shed. The need for shunters also diminished with the increasing switch to multiple units for passenger trains, to which parcels and/or fish vans were not attached, so Paragon station no longer needed one resulting in the three smaller type of Class 03 being transferred away in August 1982. Nemesis arrived on 19th January 1987, when the remaining nine Class 08 were transferred to York and Botanic was reduced to just re-fuelling, its driver signing-on point moved to Paragon station. Hull no longer had a single locomotive allocated - a sad, and unbelievable contrast to the days when 337 Hull based locomotives were taken over by the LNER on 1st January 1923, and even the 207 which British Railways nationalised on 1st January 1948.

1970	IN	CL03 2100, 2168, 2171, 2172, 2174; CL08 3070, 3074, 3075, 3077, 3079, 3080, 3081, 3232, 3233, 3234, 3236, 3313, 3318, 3323, 3675, 3676, 3944, 3945; CL11 12121 (24)
	OUT	CL08 3074; CL11 12121 (2)
1971	IN	CL03 2112, 2158 (2)
	OUT	CL03 2100, 2168, 2174; CL08 3080, 3313 (5)
1972	IN	CL03 2073; CL08 3734 (2)
	OUT	CL03 2172; CL08 3075, 3081 (3)
1973	IN	CL03 2151, 2152, 2157, 2169, 2173 (5)
	OUT	CL03 2173; CL08 3070 (2)
1974	IN	03137; 08004, 08093, 08317 (4)
	OUT	03151, 03152, 03157, 03171 (4)
1975	IN	03157; 08099 (2)
	OUT	03157, 03169; 08004, 08063, 08064 (5)
1976	IN	03063; 08435 (2)
	OUT	03137, 03158; 08093, 08514 (4)
1977	IN	(0)
	OUT	(0)
1978	IN	08514 (1)
	OUT	08164, 08513 (2)
1979	IN	(0)
	OUT	(0)
1980	IN	08008, 08061, 08440 (3)
	OUT	08008, 08165, 08435, 08514 (4)
1981	IN	08177, 08386 (2)
	OUT	08386, 08440, 08776 (3)
1982	IN	08391, 08392 (2)
	OUT	03063, 03073, 03112; 08099, 08166, 08317 (6)
1983	IN	08296, 08304 (2)
	OUT	(0)
1984	IN	08885 (1)
	OUT	08061, 08248, 08392 (3)
1985	IN	08499, 08567, 08745, 08776 (4)
	OUT	08304, 08391, 08567, 08885 (4)
1986	IN	(0)
	OUT	(0)
1987	IN	(0)
	OUT	08168, 08177, 08253, 08296, 08499, 08567, 08745, 08776, 08777 (9)

Note: Numbers in brackets indicate total movement for that year.

From 1973, renumbering to five digits began, the first two indicating classification. In 03 class the other three figures were unchanged, but at Botanic Gardens the thirteen 08 class lost their original identity thus - 3077/08063, 3079/08064, 3232/08164, 3233/08165, 3234/08166, 3236/08168, 3318/08248, 3323/08253, 3675/08513, 3676/08514, 3734/08567, 3944/08776, 3945/08777.

This Sunday 24th June 1923 photograph inside Botanic shed reveals the rather pleasing sight of immaculate class 3CC 4-4-0 no.1619 (re-classified to D19 by the LNER) alongside class A 2-4-2T no.1322 (re-classified F8 by the LNER). The 4-4-0, complete with copper capped chimney, was the sole example of its class and moved to Botanic Gardens from Leeds about 1907, staying at the Hull shed until moved to Bridlington in 1926 to work the same duties that it had nearly always worked from Paragon, the fast passenger services of the Bridlington route. Built in 1893, 1619 was withdrawn in October 1930, its long life being quite a feat for a one-off design. Tank engine 1322 has the first company insignia L. & N. E. R. on the tank side but still sports its 'A' class designation on the bufferbeam. *Authors collection.*

Sentinel 2-cylinder railcars were associated with Botanic Gardens shed from 1927 until October 1946 when the last one was withdrawn. Better known by their names than their fleet numbers, the railcars were a common sight around Hull and there was always at least five of them allocated to Botanic from 1928 onwards. Here No.29 ROCKINGHAM, surrounded by piles of ash and clinker, moves away from the coal stage which had been kept for their sole use, at some unknown date. *Authors collection.*

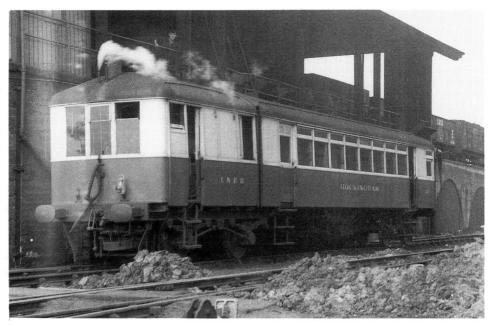

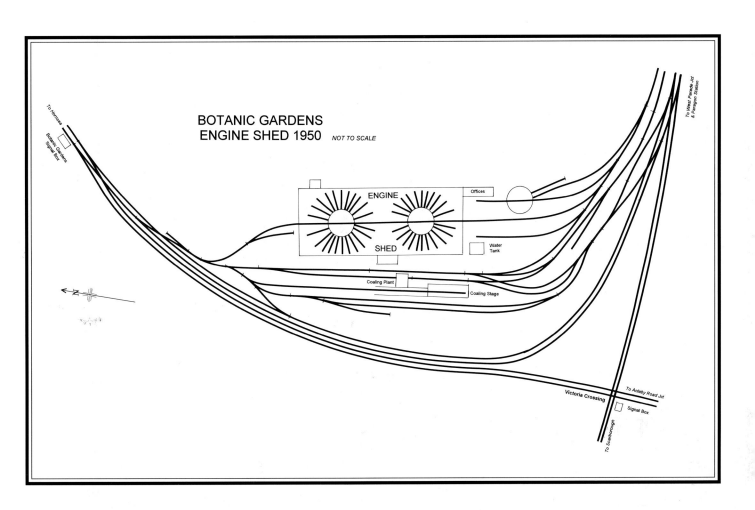

**BOTANIC GARDENS
ENGINE SHED 1950** *NOT TO SCALE*

ENGINE

SHED

Offices

Water
Tank

Coaling Plant

Coaling Stage

To Hornsea

Botanic Gardens
Signal Box

To West Parade Jct
& Paragon Station

Victoria Crossing

To Anlaby Road Jct

Signal Box

To Scarborough

(left) **A pre-war view of the Botanic coaler. Costing in excess of £6,200 when built in 1932, the coaler was equipped with a single bunker which held what might be described as 'good quality coal' for the use of passenger engines. Many of these large concrete coaling plants were erected throughout the country during the 1930's and were of varying capacities and usually had at least two storage bunkers for different grades of coal. Botanic being responsible solely for passenger train work had therefore the need of only one such bunker.** *Authors collection.*

(below) **The North Eastern Railway built 110 of the Worsdell designed Class O 0-4-4T between 1894 and 1901. All passed into LNER ownership and were re-classified G5. They could be found in all parts of the former NER and Hull was no exception. 2098 was photographed on Botanic shed yard at some time in 1933 during its 1929-34 allocation there.** *Authors collection.*

Six of Thompson's new L1 tank locomotives arrived at Botanic in 1948 followed by five more during the following year however five of the original six left the shed to bring the balance back to six. This arrangement went on until 1956 when the last ones departed. There was never more than seven at any one time allocated to Botanic where they performed on the Doncaster, Pontefact, Hornsea, Withernsea and Brough passenger services. 67719 was one of the 1948 arrivals and is shown in the then green livery afforded these engines. *Authors collection.*

For many years Botanic shed supplied most of the Paragon station shunting pilots (Dairycoates supplied the rest). Today however with the advent of HST's on the London service and the universal use of diesel multiple units on all the remaining services, the need for shunting pilots has ceased. Fouteen years ago it was quite different, when Class O3 and O8 diesel shunters were employed and on the 28th August 1981, outside Botanic shed, 03073 awaits its next 'Paragon pilot' duty. The locomotives 'washed-out' look was due to its numerous trips through the nearby carriage washing plant. *53A Models, Hull.*

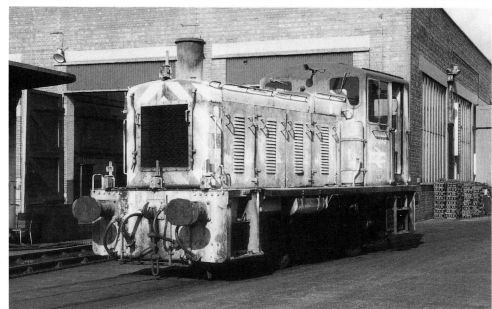

This was the scene inside Botanic Gardens shed in December 1987 - almost pristine compared with previous steam-era interior views. The Class 101 two-car d.m.u., was a typical first generation unit used extensively on local services. Standing alongside the east wall of the shed, the unit is positioned in what was the old No.1 shed whilst beyond would have been the No.2 shed. The difference in roof heights indicates the demarkation. Alongside the running rails are removeable floor grilles which allow any fluid spillage to drain safely into underground sumps. *Steve Jordan.*

THE ENGINE SHED AT CHALK LANE STORE YARD

At the opposite side of Hessle Road crossing to Dairycoates shed, and about the same distance away, the Hull District Engineer had an extensive store yard for rails and other permanent way materials. There were sixteen sidings, some of them almost 300 yards long, but it was not until 1955 that a shunting engine was allocated specifically to it, unlike the corresponding yards at York and Darlington, which had their own Departmental locomotives. Traffic to and from the Chalk Lane yard, and the movement of wagons in it, was done by engines in Capital Stock allocated to Dairycoates shed. For example, in 1951 their Trip No.23B worked traffic to Store Yard after it had prepared the 7.30 a.m. to Hornsea, and the 7.50 a.m. to Withernsea pick-up goods trains. Then Trip No.17 engine arrived at 9.00 a.m. to shunt the

Yard as needed *(see page 78 for list of Authorised Pilot and Shunting engines)*.

Until 1929 it is believed that the shunting in the yard was done mainly by one of the five 0-4-0 locomotives of class Y8, all of which were shedded at Dairycoates from new in 1890 until 1936 or later. From the 1930's, some of that work was taken over by the Y1 class Sentinel shunting engines, which could be operated by single manning instead of needing a driver and a fireman, thereby reducing the cost appreciably. Dairycoates usually had three of them, but by 1954/55 they were reaching the end of their economic life, so in March 1955 British Railways purchased an 88 h.p. 4-wheel diesel mechanical shunting locomotive from Ruston & Hornsby, put it into non-revenue earning stock as Departmental Locomotive No.56 and

allocated it specifically to Chalk Lane Yard, and not to Dairycoates as all its predecessors had been. It is understood that a wood shed was provided to house it, but in 1963 it was transferred away, and Chalk Lane Store Yard was gradually run down, much of its site now being occupied by housing.

The title of Chalk Lane for the yard was something of a misnomer because between the yard and that lane were two very busy main railway lines, the one to and from Paragon station and the goods line between Hessle Road and Cottingham Junctions. The employees' entrance and that for any road vehicles was in Haltemprice Street, one of Chalk Lane's side streets, and on to which butted the end of the Stores Shed shown in our illustration, also the Time Office.

Departmental Locomotive No.56 outside the store shed in Chalk Lane yard in which it worked from new in March 1955 until transferred to Bishop Auckland in 1963. The tiny shunter was the first of seven such shunters supplied to the North Eastern Region of BR between 1955 and 1961 to carry out work in the various depots run by the Civil and Mechanical Engineering departments. Immediately to the rear of the cab can be seen the back end of one of the Sentinel steam shunters which the diesel displaced. In addition to stores, this corrugated iron shed also provided shelter for the mobile crane used for lifting lengths of rail, which explains the height of the entrance. *Mike Lake.*

THE TWO ENGINE SHEDS AT PARAGON STATION

The movement of the passenger trains from Manor House to Paragon station, which was opened without any ceremony in May 1848, needed accommodation there for the engines, and on the north side of the station, adjacent to the arrival platform, that was provided by a three-road shed about 125 feet long, the tendering price for which was £2100. Just ahead of the front of the shed was a turntable of 45 feet diameter. Then in 1854, the York & North Midland joined up with the York, Newcastle & Berwick, also the Leeds Northern, to form the very powerful North Eastern Railway, and the three-road shed at Paragon was soon quite inadequate to deal with just the passenger engines based on that station. So an additional shed was

authorised in 1865, and after further authorisation more than doubled its size, that Paragon shed became operative in 1867. Within ten years, another extension, this time a square 'roundhouse' to take twenty engines was built on land just to the north of the station coal depot and some distance from the original straight shed. Typical of the standard North Eastern Railway 3-bay roundhouse of the period, the north wall of the new shed was bounded by St Stephen's Square. The central turntable gave access to twenty radiating roads each with its own inspection pit.

In 1897 the N.E.R. decided to enlarge Paragon station considerably, and the Locomotive Department were informed that would require the

complete removal of the two Paragon sheds. In consequence, Botanic Gardens shed came to be built, and immediately it became operative in 1901, a contractor's tender of £384 for the demolition of the 3-road straight shed was accepted in May 1901, it is not known if this amount included demolition of the roundhouse as well. Work on that part of the station could then go ahead and the three rebuilt bays, and the two new ones on the north side were opened on December 12th 1904, putting the station structure much as most of us have known it. The addition of the two extra bays involved the sweeping away of the three-road shed which had been an integral part of the original Paragon station buildings stemming from 1848.

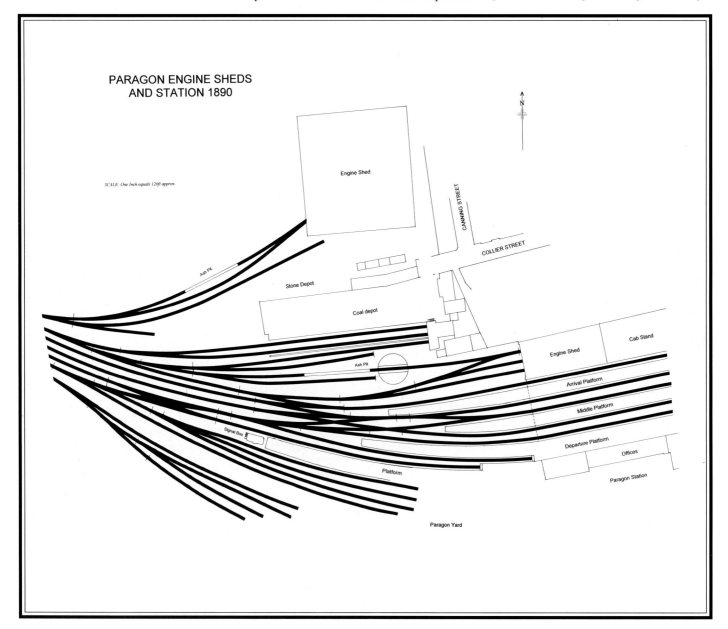

PARAGON ENGINE SHEDS
AND STATION 1890

SCALE: One Inch equals 120ft approx.

THE ENGINE SHED AT HULL'S VICTORIA STATION

That station was situated between Victoria Dock and the Hedon Road, just to the east of Drypool. It was built, and owned jointly by the Hull & Holderness Railway, and the York & North Midland Railway; it opened on 24th June 1854, only five weeks prior to the Y&NM being taken in to the North Eastern Railway. For its Hull station the Holderness line was granted power to use the Victoria Dock branch from a junction that it made with it near to Southcoates, the original intention being that the York & North Midland would work the line to and from Withernsea. Until February 1857 the Holderness line did hire power from them, and the engines concerned would be from the 3-road shed integral with Paragon station, but then decided to work the line themselves. They bought a small tank engine for £620 from the North British Railway, but it proved a bad bargain, because in October 1857 they had to send it to its makers, R.& W.Hawthorn in Newcastle for repairs which cost them another £137. It

returned to Hull in January 1858, and in its absence, they must have had to continue hiring from the North Eastern. Soon appreciating that their secondhand engine was unreliable, the Holderness directors ordered a new engine from Kitson, in Leeds, which was delivered in April 1858 and cost £2250. To house their own two engines, in May 1858, the building of a shed for £140 was ordered, which appears to have been about 30 feet long from what was shown on a map of 1861 and was most probably of timber construction, over one line of track. Then in an Act dated July 7th 1862, the North Eastern gained the absorption of the Hull & Holderness Railway, and with the installation of a curve at Southcoates, Withernsea trains were able to work to, and from Paragon station. The shed at Victoria Dock was thereby made redundant, and is believed to have been taken down to be re-erected as the goods warehouse at Lockington, north of Beverley on the Bridlington line, in June 1866.

The Holderness line's two engines were re-numbered into North Eastern stock as 415 and 416 in 1862, but the secondhand engine (415) was regarded only as scrap, and was quickly cut up. The 1858 built engine then worked a life of almost twenty years, its number 416 being cleared for re-use in December 1878 on a 0-4-4 tank engine of the BTP class.

So ends the survey of engine sheds that have served the railways of Hull. Only Botanic Gardens is still operational but for how long - and now, no motive power is allocated to it.

An undated photograph of the NER square 'roundhouse' at Paragon station. The view was probably captured shortly before the shed was vacated for demolition as the immediate surroundings appear to be untidy even for an engine shed. There was only one entrance/exit for engines at this shed which, as can be seen, was at an angle to the main axis of the building. One of the advantages of a roundhouse shed is that the entrance can be placed anywhere in the walls of the building even, as at Dairycoates, in a corner. Engines could be watered on their way into the shed without blocking the approach road as a by-pass line was available for engines leaving the shed. Coaling still had to be carried out at the wooden stage near the old 3-road shed.
British Railways.

Station or Yard	Shed provided by	Number	Period required	Particulars of Work
Albert Dock	Dairycoates	10	0600 to 2200 SX	
			0600 to 1400 SO	Shunts on Albert Dock. Works trips Inward Yard to Albert Dock, Albert Dock to Outward Yard and as required.
Albert Dock	Dairycoates	11	0605 to 2200 Wd	Works coal and coke empties to and from Albert Dock and as required.
Alexandra Dock	Alexandra Dock	50	0600 M to 0600 Su	Shunting as required.
Alexandra Dock	Alexandra Dock	51	0800 to 1600 SX	Shunting as required.
Alexandra Dock	Alexandra Dock	53	0600 M to 0600 Su	Shunting as required.
Alexandra Dock	Alexandra Dock	54	0600 M to 0600 Su	Shunting as required.
Alexandra Dock	Alexandra Dock	55	0600 M to 0600 Su	Shunting as required.
Alexandra Dock	Alexandra Dock	56	0600 to 2200 Wd	Shunting as required.
Alexandra Dock	Alexandra Dock	57	0600 M to 0600 Su	Shunting as required.
Alexandra Dock	Alexandra Dock	58	0600 M to 0600 Su	Shunting as required.
Alexandra Dock	Alexandra Dock	59	0600 M to 0600 Su	Shunting as required.
Dairycoates	Dairycoates	7	0530 to 2120 Wd	Works two trips Inward Yard to Manor House; breakfast; Belle Vue to Inward Yard; 1230 trip Inward Yard to Manor House. Shunts Old Creek; weighs traffic at Found Out. Works 1830 trip Manor House to Outward Yard. Then works for Dairycoates Inspector to 2120.
Dairycoates	Dairycoates	19	0725 M to 0530 Su	Works as required by Dairycoates Inspector.
Dairycoates	Dairycoates	23b	0040 M to 2200 Sa	Works Humps Inward Yard to Outward Yard. Prepares 0750 Withernsea, 0730 Hornsea pickups. Works traffic to Chalk Lane Storeyard, shunts there until 1230. Works as required by Dairycoates Inspector.
Dairycoates Shed	Dairycoates	19a	0800 to 1600 Wd	Shunting as required.
Drypool	Dairycoates	24	0600 to 2200 Wd	Shunting as required.
Drypool	Dairycoates	24a	1300 to 2100 SX	
			0800 to 1600 SO	Shunting as required.
Drypool	Dairycoates	25	0600 to 2200 Wd	Shunting as required.
Drypool	Dairycoates	27	0600 to 2200 Wd	Shunting as required.
Drypool	Dairycoates	28	0600 to 2200 Wd	Shunting as required.
Goole	Botanic Gardens	—	1930 to 2200 Wd	Shunt at Goole. Work 2210 Class H Goole - Hull.
Inward Yard	Dairycoates	18	0700 to 1300 MO	
			1500 to 2145 Wd	
			2215 to 1300 SX	
			2215 Sa to 0600 Su	Shunting on Inward Hump.
Inwards Yard	Dairycoates	20	1230 to 2100 Wd	Shunting and preparing Branch trains and transferring.
King George Dock	Alexandra Dock	91	0600 M to 0600 Su	Shunting as required.
King George Dock	Alexandra Dock	92	0600 M to 0600 Su	Shunting as required.
King George Dock	Alexandra Dock	93	0600 M to 0600 Su	Shunting as required.
King George Dock	Alexandra Dock	94	0600 M to 0600 Su	Shunting as required.
King George Dock	Alexandra Dock	95	0600 M to 0600 Su	Shunting as required.
King George Dock	Alexandra Dock	96	0600 M to 0600 Su	Shunting as required.
King George Dock	Alexandra Dock	97	0600 M to 0600 Su	Shunting as required
King George Dock	Alexandra Dock	99	0600 to 2200 Wd	Shunting and tripping between King George Dock and Salt End.
Manor House Yard	Dairycoates	1	0800 to 2359 SX	
			0610 to 2200 SO	Shunts at Manor House. Works 1620 trip Manor House to Inward Yard. Humps Inward Yard to Outward Yard. Mineral empties Inward Yard to Empty Mineral. Hull goods from Empty Mineral and St James' Street, Landsale, from Laden Mineral. Shunts Old Creek 1300 SO.
Manor House	Dairycoates	2	0550 M to 0600 Su	Shunts Manor House yard. Runs LE at 0200 to Inward Yard for Hulls to Manor House yard.
Manor House	Dairycoates	3	0555 to 2200 M - F	
			0555 to 1400 SO	Shunts Manor House yard. Works Outward Yard goods Manor House to Neptune Street N.E. at 1230 and 1620 Q.
Mineral Yard	Dairycoates	40	1250 M to 2200 Sa	Shunting at Empty Sidings
Mineral Yard	Dairycoates	42	0600 to 2330 Wd	Shunts at Old Priory, Empty and Laden Sidings as required. Relieve No.44 Pilot for Loco. duties 2200 to 2330.
Neptune Street N.E.	Dairycoates	6	0700 to 2300 SX	
			0615 to 2200 SO	Shunts English Street and Neptune Street N.E. Yards.
Neptune Street H.B.	Dairycoates	62	0500 to 2100 Wd	Shunting Neptune Street H.B. and preparing pick-ups.
Old Priory	Dairycoates	44	0600 M to 0600 Su	Shunts at Old Priory, Empty and Laden Sidings as required. Relieved by No.42 Pilot for Loco. duties 2200 to 2330 Wd.
Outward Yard	Dairycoates	12	0600 M to 0600 Su	Shunts at Outward Yard West End.
Outward Yard	Dairycoates	15	0115 M to 2200 Sa	Marshalling traffic and preparing loads in Outward Yard. Takes Fish traffic to Outward Yard.
Outward Yard	Dairycoates	16	1400 to 0600 SX	
			1300 Sa to 0600 Su	Shunting on Outward Yard Hump.
Outward Yard	Dairycoates	17	0900 M to 0600 Su	Shunts Chalk Lane Yard at 0900. Then works trips Outward Yard to Inward Yard and return. Shunts at West End Outward Yard.
Outward Yard	Dairycoates	17a	0735 to 2335 SX	
			0635 to 2235 SO	(1) Fish empties. Inward Yard to Old Inward Yard or as required by Dairycoates Inspector. (2) 0900 Old Inward Yard, shunting and pre-testing. (3) 1700 Outward Yard pre-testing. 1830 York. (4) 1830 shunt Ledgers Sidings and Chalk Lane. (5) 2100 Chalk Lane to Inward Yard.
Paragon	Botanic Gardens	33	0200 to 1930 Wd	Shunting as required
Paragon	Dairycoates	34	0500 M to 0830 Su	Shunting as required
Paragon	Botanic Gardens	35	0525 M to 0200 Su	Shunting as required
St. Andrew's Dock	Dairycoates	21	0600 to 2200 Wd	Shunting South Side St. Andrew's Dock and West End Outward Yard. Prepares 2050 East Goods. Clears fish kits from Outward Yard.
St. Andrew's Dock	Dairycoates	21a	0610 M to 0600 Su	Working coal and coal empties to and from St. Andrew's Dock.
St. Andrew's Dock	Dairycoates	22	0110 M to 2200 Sa	Sets St. Andrew's Dock with fish empties. C&W 1300. Shunts on St. Andrew's Dock until after departure of 1730 Guide Bridge fish. Marshals trains at West End Outward Yard.
St. Andrew's Dock	Dairycoates	22a	0800 to 2359 SX	
			0600 to 2200 SO	Assisting with fish traffic and dealing with fish empties.
Stepney	Botanic Gardens	123Sentinel	0600 to 2000 Wd	Shunting as required.
Springhead	Springhead	76	0600 to 2000 Wd	Shunting Landsale traffic and Co-operative Depot.
Springhead	Springhead	77	0600 to 2130 MO	
			2300 to 2130 M-F	
			2300 Sa to 1800 Su	Shunting, disposing of Inward trains and preparing loads. Takes loco coal into loco yard on completion of work SO.
Springhead	Springhead	78	0700 to 1800 SX	Shunting for Springhead C&W Department. Takes loco coal into loco yard on completion of work SX.
Victoria Dock	Dairycoates	124Sentinel	0700 to 1700 SX	
			0700 to 1200 SO	Shunting as required.
Wilmington	Botanic Gardens	38	0500 to 2100 Wd	Shunting as required.

Key: M - Monday; M-F - Monday to Friday; MO - Monday Only; Sa - Saturday; SO - Saturday Only; Su - Sunday; SX - Saturday Excepted; Wd - weekdays.

Former NER N8 0-6-2T 959 works one of the Albert Dock turns in 1932. Pilot No.10 was required to trip between Albert Dock and Outwards Yard and return from Inwards Yard besides shunting on the dock between 6.00 a.m. and 10.00 p.m. Mondays to Friday. Dairycoates supplied the engine.

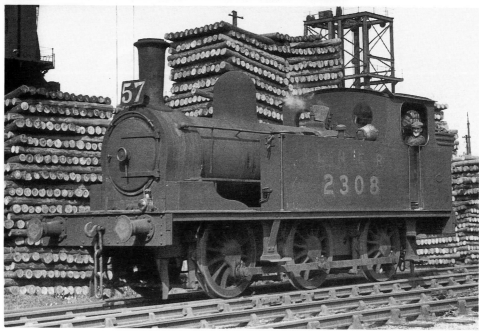

Surrounded by pit props the crew of J72 2308 seem a happy pair whilst awaiting the next shunting job at Alexandra Dock in September 1938. For working in the prop yards, the engines had to be equipped with spark arresters but that particular piece of equipment seems to be missing from 2308.

There were two pilot jobs carried out by Sentinel locomotives in Hull, 123 and 124. Here a filthy 68182 working pilot 124 from Dairycoates shed in April 1956 is at Victoria Dock, almost entirely for moving wagons of timber.

Authors collection.

LOCAL TRIP WORKINGS

41262 was the only Ivatt 2-6-2T to be allocated to Dairycoates. Arriving in February 1960, it did much useful work in the Hull area until it was transferred away to Warrington in November 1963. Here passing Dairycoates East signal box on 27th September 1962, 41262 is making its way back to shed on the No.1 Up Goods line after working local trip J22. *Ian K.Watson.*

Once upon a time.....Hull was a major fishing port, and St Andrews Dock, referred to locally as "The Fish Dock", was a constant scene of activity. This late 1950's view has J25 65693 preparing to shunt fish vans into a train for an afternoon trip working to Outward Yard. Road vehicles had already begun to take much of the fish traffic away from the railway and with the eventual decline of the fish trade in general and the opening of motorways the days of the fish trains were numbered. *N.E.stead.*

A double headed train near or within the city was something of a rare event, and then, as if in a final act of defiance, for the last few months of steam working we were treated to such a scene on an almost daily basis. This involved what would now be called a 'Block Load' of tank wagons, and originated at the Saltend refinery. Some contemporary railwaymen referred to these wagons as "Big Tanks", this is simply and quite logically explained because they were bigger then anything that had come before them. Regretfully views of this working seem to be almost non-existent, and we make no excuses for offering this rather evocative picture of two unknown, but local WD 2-8-0s working off King George Dock. The date is Wednesday 11th January 1967, and with the leading engine now almost on level ground the train is about to cross the Hedon Road bridge. It will then proceed toward Southcoates station and the Victoria Dock branch, then onward across the city for eventual forwarding to the West Riding. The three arm signal seen on the right was erected by BR to replace the original NER three doll bracket on 24th June 1954. The arms read as follows: top - No.25 Shunting Down NER Mineral to Coal Sidings No.1; middle - No.27 Shunting Down NER Mineral; bottom - No.32 Shunting Down NER Mineral to Coal Sidings No.2. *The Rev. David Benson.*

(below) It was more usual for the Type 1 Diesels or "Camels" as they were often referred to locally, to work in tandem. The leading or pilot engine which had arrived here from Canton on 9th January 1967 is D9546, whilst the train engine, D9515, also a former Canton engine had arrived in Hull a day earlier. Both engines were eventually withdrawn from Dairycoates shed on 1st April 1968, and then sold for further use to industry during the November of that year. The lead engine is not carrying headlamps, and the 4-character headcode indicator shows an incorrect display, when used correctly the code 0J06 would refer either to a light engine or two or more engines coupled, and clearly this is not the case here. The view of Botanic Station or more correctly its environs was taken on Monday 8th May 1967 or some two and half years after the withdrawal of the Hornsea and Withernsea passenger services. Even so, and as the well polished railheads show the former Up and Down passenger lines are still in use, but only just, and within a matter of weeks the Up Main Points over which the train engine is passing would be "spiked out of use pending removal". Totally obscuring the level crossing is a typical cast iron standard NER footbridge, several of which to this day remain in use, but alas not within the City of Hull. Peeping out behind the leading engine can just be seen Botanic Gardens signal box which had first been brought into use during the summer of 1881, inspected by the BoT on 29th July of that year. Following the work involved with the commencement of the new Botanic Gardens engine shed in 1898 it became necessary to increase the length of the signal box, and at the same time to work both the existing and additional connections, a new locking frame, consisting of two gate wheels and 39 levers was installed. Visible behind the footbridge are the premises of Wilfred Fairburn Ltd. Electrical Engineers, Contractors and Armature Winders, these still stand today, and have only recently been vacated by this long established local company. Following the decline of the railway, Wilfred Fairburn expanded his works westwards, and eventually occupied most of the old station area. This too is now sold off, and from November 1994 became the site of the Old Zoological public house. *The Rev.David Benson.*

SIGNALLING AND SIGNAL BOXES WITHIN THE HULL AREA

Signalling in a very basic form has existed since the coming of the railways. By the mid 1870s "modern" signalling had come about and railway companies started to convert their systems. The North Eastern Railway, in line with all the other major railways, was introducing "Block Working" and providing signal boxes as we would recognise them today. It is this period in time that has been chosen as the commencement date in the main table of signal boxes that once existed within the boundaries of Hull.

Although none of the 1870s type of signal boxes remain within the city, there are several working examples from this period to be found just outside the boundary, notably at Crabley Creek to the west of Brough, and at Driffield.

On the 29th November 1872 the North Eastern Railway carried out a survey which refers to a total of eighteen signal boxes within the area covered in this book and these, with their status noted alongside, were as follows:-

ANLABY ROAD - Locking on order.

CEMETERY GATES STATION - Not locked and no plan.
CEMETERY JUNCTION - Interlocked.
COTTINGHAM JUNCTION - Not locked and no plan.
HESSLE JUNCTION - Interlocked.
HESSLE ROAD - Interlocked.
HULL DAIRYCOATES JCT - Not locked and no plan.
HULL GOODS JCT - Not locked and no plan.
HULL STATION - Not locked and no plan.
MARFLEET - Not locked and no plan.
SCULCOATES STATION - Locking on order.
SOUTHCOATES STATION & JCT - Interlocked.
STEPNEY STATION - Not locked and no plan.
SUTTON - Not locked and no plan.
VICTORIA CROSSING - Not locked and no plan.
VICTORIA DOCK - Not locked and no plan.
WEST PARADE - Interlocked.
WILMINGTON STATION & JCT - Interlocked.

Looking west through Anlaby Road gates on a fine and now long forgotten Edwardian summer's day. Apart from a few detail changes this view was destined to remain much the same for the best part of 60 years and the coming of the flyover in 1964. The first alterations would be about 1925 when the three 'splitting distants' were taken out of use and removed from the signal bridge. Things would then probably remain much the same until the withdrawal of the trams on 5th September 1942. This would be the only significant change apparent to the layman, even so this would not happen overnight, and it would be some time before the tram rails were recovered. Though its unlikely the gates were the originals, these, by their very nature, had a somewhat high mortality rate, and would from time to time need replacing usually as a result of 'a run through'. In comparison with our view of Walton Street *(see page 94)* the telegraph pole with its eight line arms seen through the gates, indicates the Hull Corporation Telephone Department is doing a fair business in the immediate area. There are also two poles on railway land just to the south of the crossing and although both of these may be in Company use this is not necessarily the case for it was the practice of the GPO to erect their 'Trunk Routes' alongside the railway. As an aside its also worth mentioning that the H&BR by the use of the signalbox telegraph actually transmitted and received GPO telegrams for the public. There is much to interest the railway modeller in this picture. He may like to note the intricate scroll work on the tramway standard, and the stay rods on the gates and their posts. The smaller of the main gates may be of standard length i.e. 14 feet, whilst the larger one will not be less than 30 feet. Close inspection reveals the 'gate stops' to be in the 'four foot' of the west or outward bound tram lines. Other points to note are the four gas lights, one on each corner of the crossing, and also the way the railway company's telegraph wires are bound into a cable whilst passing over the level crossing. This was standard practice when other electric cables were involved, in this case the conductors of the Corporation Tramway Department. *Memory Lane Hull.*

HULL AREA SIGNALBOXES to 1995.

HULL & BARNSLEY MAIN LINE

Signalbox	Frame Type	GW	Lvrs	Opened	Closed	Type	Remarks
King George Dock	M&H 16 App	—	90	26/6/14	28/5/74	S4	Levers 61-90 never used. Originally known as Joint Dock Jct. Property of Joint Dock Committee. Frame shortened to 60 levers probably 10/11/41.
Holderness Drain	E.O.D.	—	50	26/6/14	12/73	HB 1	Renamed by LNER Holderness Drain South
Alexandra Dock East	?	—	—	1904?	—	—	Originally a GF then became Graving Dock
Graving Dock	E.O.D	—	40	1/10/20	27/7/68	HB 1	Ready 1/4/15. Opening delayed by Great War
Graving Dock GF	GF	—	10	1/10/20	—	—	—
Alexandra Dock	S&F Rocker	?	48	20/7/85	1910	SF 10	—
Alexandra Dock	E.O.D.	1	88	1910	1920s	HB 1	—
Alexandra Dock (FE)	E.O.D.	1	97	1920s	8/58	HB 1	—
Alexandra Dock (RF)	M&H 17 App	1	91	8/58	28/5/74	HB 1	GW removed 1/7/66 and boom gates installed.
Bridges Junction	E.O.D.	—	25	1914	-/11/38	HB 1	—
Bridges Junction GF	GF	—	6	24/2/42	2/11/50	HB 1	Provision of emergency route in case of enemy action
Burleigh Street GF	covered GF	—	2	9/1897	1906	—	Provision of Up coal sidings. released by lock & block
Burleigh Street	E.O.D.	—	17	1906	2/1/65	HB 1	—
Burleigh Street GF	BR Std.GF	—	?	2/1/65	-/4/73	EGF	Worked mains cross-over
Burleigh Street GF	BR Std.GF	—	?	2/1/65	-/4/73	EGF	Worked BOCM siding
Hull Bridge	S&F Rocker	—	13	20/7/85	1931	Spec.	Closed as a Block Post
Hull Bridge	?	—	?	1931	3/1/64	Reb.	Now not a Block Post
Hull Bridge	S&F + panel	—	6	3/1/64	S.I.U.	Reb	Provision of Switch panel for signals only
Sculcoates Junction	S&F Rocker	—	29	20/7/85	4/10/54	SF 10	—
Sculcoates Junction (RF)	M&H 16 App	—	30	4/10/54	4/5/68	SF 10	—
Sculcoates Down GF	?	—	4	1961	27/11/72	EGF	Worked cross-over and Gas siding. Down side
Sculcoates CEGB GF	?	—	2	4/5/68	?	EGF	Works CEGB siding
Beverley Road	S&F Rocker	—	35	20/7/85	1931	SF 10	—
Beverley Road GF	?	—	2	?	?	EGF	—
Cannon Street	S&F Rocker	—	35	20/7/85	-/10/24	SF 10	Possibly retained as GF. Still standing o.o.u. c1948
Cannon Street GF	?	—	?	?	-/1/56	?	—
Ella Street	E.O.D.	—	13	10/8/03	5/10/37	HB 1	—
Ella Street GF	?	—	2	5/10/37	7/2/72	EGF	Released from Springbank N., worked Down siding
Springbank North	S&F Rocker	—	26	20/7/85	29/6/24	SF 10	Later 27 levers
Springbank North	M&H 16 App	—	45	29/6/24	4/5/68	S 4	Provision of new junction to NE Section
Locomotive Jct	S&F Rocker	—	40	20/7/85	-/9/13	SF 10	—
Locomotive Jct (RF)	E.O.D.	—	50	-/9/13	13/5/45	SF 10	—
Locomotive Jct (RF)	M&H 16 App	—	45	13/5/45	7/11/64	SF 10	Worked as a GF until 11/11/64

HULL & BARNSLEY NEPTUNE STREET BRANCH

Signalbox	Frame Type	GW	Lvrs	Opened	Closed	Type	Remarks
Neptune Street	E.O.D.	—	50	1897	—	HB 1	—
(Neptune St) Subway	E.O.D.	—	50	1923	—	HB 1	Renamed by LNER
Subway (FE)	E.O.D.	—	60	1928	29/1/38	HB 1	Closed on provision of new LNER Albert Dock box
Subway "B" GF	S&F	—	12	20/7/85	1931	?	—
Subway "A" GF	S&F	—	12	20/7/85	1897		Closed on provision of new Neptune St box
Subway	S&F Rocker	—	?	20/7/85	1897	SF 10	Closed on provision of new Neptune St box
Liverpool Street	E.O.D.	—	22	25/6/14	15/10/26	HB 1	Destroyed by fire. Out of regular use from 1915
Boothferry Park GF	BR Std.GF	—	2	30/8/65	S.I.U.	EGF	—
Springbank South	S&F Rocker	—	17	20/7/85	1/3/44	SF 10	—

Neptune Street box, in October 1964, originated from the late 1870s and the provision of both basic signalling and "Block Working" much as we understand it today. Records of this installation are incomplete, and from an historical point of view leave a lot to be desired. Interestingly what remains tells us that at one time the locking frame consisted of 51 levers, these being a mixture of Saxby & Farmer and NER apparatus, and perhaps surprisingly to modern thinking, without interlocking. It seems this state of affairs was allowed to remain until 1933 when the LNER provided a new frame of 40 levers with full interlocking. Even today the provision of interlocking and signalling on purely "Goods Only" lines is not mandatory, but only a recommendation. *John Foreman.*

NEPTUNE STREET BRANCH cont.

Springbank South (RF)	M&H 16 App	—	20	1/3/44	4/5/68	SF 10	—
Springbank West	S&F Rocker	—	?	20/7/85	1901	SF 10	—
Springbank West (RF)	E.O.D.	—	40	1901	5/2/23	SF 10	—
Springbank West	E.O.D.	—	40	5/2/23	14/5/44	HB	1901 frame from old box possibly re-used
Springbank West (RF)	M&H 17 App	—	45	14/5/44	7/11/64	HB	—
Springbank West No.2	E.O.D.	—	25	1/7/08	1938	HB 1	Not a Block Post
Springhead Sidings	E.O.D.	—	25	1938	7/5/44	HB 1	Springbank West No.2 box renamed. Replaced by a GF but never brought into use, became handpoints
Springhead GF	?	—	?	9/13	13/11/28	CGF	Points/sigs worked from Loco Jct box from 13/11/28

HULL YARDS

MINERAL YARD

Coal Siding West	?	—	?	?	1905	?	—
Coal Siding West	?	—	?	1905	5/1908	S 2	—
Coal Siding West (FE) (C.S.W.)	?	—	77	5/1908	—	S 2	—
St Andrew's Dock West	?	—	82	?	—	S 2	Coal Sidings West renamed and frame extended ?
St Andrew's Dock	?	—	55	31/10/38	23/7/66	S 2	St.A.D.W. renamed 31/10/38
No.1 Section	M&H 16 App	—	35	1905	?	?	8' 0", 20' 9" x 9' 6"
Middle Section	M&H 11 App	—	50	?	?	?	8' 6", 30' 0" x 19' 9"

MARSHALLING YARD

No.1	?	—	?	?	?	?	—
No.2	?	—	9	?	1909	?	—
No.3	?	—	8	?	?	?	—
Albert Dock West	S&F App	—	33	?	26/4/08	?	Frame re-locked with tappets 1896. 8' 6", 25' 0" x 12' 0"
Albert Dock West (RF)	M&H 16 App	—	40	26/4/08	27/2/37	?	—
No.4	?	—	?	?	?	?	—
No.8 Section	?	—	?	1908	1914	?	—

GOODS & DOCK LINES

New Engine Shed Jct	M&H 6 App	—	30	1891	6/1906	?	9' 9", 10' 0" x 26' 0". Believed to be same location as Dairycoates Eng Shed box. First appears in appendix of Feb 1892. Listed 1/1/1904. Closed half year ending 6/1906.
Dairycoates Eng Shed	?	—	?	?	?	?	see above
Coal Sidings East	?	—	?	?	?	S 1	—
Coal Sidings East (RF)	M&H 16 App	—	55	1904	1909	S 1	9' 6", 8' 0" x 36' 2". Original box enlarged
Coal Sidings East (FE)	M&H 16 App	—	78	1909	—	S 1	—
St Andrew's Dock Jct	M&H 16 App	—	78	—	29/10/38	S 1	Coal Sidings East renamed, date unknown
Dairycoates Jct	M&H 6 App + NER App	—	34	?	-/11/06	S 1	9' 6", 8' 6" x 23' 6". Frame installed 1888
Dairycoates Jct	M&H 16 App	—	90	-/11/06	—	S 4	12' 0", 8' 6" x 50' 0".
Dairycoates Jct (FE)	M&H 16 App	—	100	—	—	S 4	—
Dairycoates East	M&H 16 App	—	100	—	—	S 4	Dairycoates Jct renamed.
Dairycoates East (FE)	M&H 16 App	—	145	—	—	S 4	LNER records of 1925 show 145 levers
Dairycoates East (FE)	M&H 16 App	—	146	—	23/7/67	S 4	Lever 70A added at unknown date
Albert Dock East	?	—	?	?	?	S 1	—

Hessle East signal box, seen here in October 1964, originated in the late months of 1904 when it was called Hessle Junction or as it was referred to in some of the NER records Hessle New Junction. Originally a locking frame of 47 levers was in use but this was later extended, first probably during 1907 when a BoT inspection of 6th September records a frame of 55 levers. This incidentally was in connection with alterations to the Goods line Junctions and the former Down Goods Independent (the line nearest the box in this view) being made suitable for passenger traffic. Then either late in 1910 or early 1911 the frame was again extended, this time to 65 levers and was certainly the case when on 23rd February 1911 the BoT inspected some new points and signals on the lines leading to Coal Sidings West. Presumably at this date the signal box itself was also extended, at the far end of the box and is visible here. At the same time a completely new wooden top was provided, this is self evident by the mixing of the two styles of architecture, the lower brick work and the arch top locking room windows belong to the S2 design type contemporary from circa 1903 to 1907, whilst the upper works are of the later and final S4 pattern. The access steps are a modern replacement and date from the early BR period. The signalman is Gavin Bricklebank. *John Foreman.*

A level crossing had existed at Dansom Lane since the opening of the Victoria branch in 1853 although it was early 1904 before a signal box was provided. Previously the gates had been worked by a crossing keeper whose domestic accommodation, in the form of the two railway cottages, can be seen on the left. The signal box is of the interim 'S2' design, only a handful of which were built, and certainly this was the only example on the Victoria Dock branch. The signal box was closed in December 1968 and swept away by the tide of rationalisation. Today one would be hard pressed to realise that a railway had existed here at all. Note the Gill Sans lettering.
Ian K. Watson.

GOODS & DOCK LINES cont.

Albert Dock East (RF)	M&H 4 App	—	21	29/5/04	—	S 1	Secondhand App ex Staddlethorpe
Albert Dock East (FE)	M&H 4 App	—	26	—	—	S 1	LNER records of 1925 show 26 levers
Albert Dock East (RF)*	?	—	?	—	29/1/38	S 1	Frame renewed or extended. 40 levers in use 1/3/37
Albert Dock	M&H 16 App	—	90	31/1/38	18/11/75	LNE	—
Foreshore	NER App	—	15	1888	7/7/31	?	—
Foreshore GF	?	—	4	?	27/11/55	?	No mention in NER records
Albert Dock GF	?	—	4	?	?	EGF	—
Neptune Street	S&F + NER	—	51	?	1933	S 1	No interlocking
Neptune Street (RF)	M&H 16 App	—	40	1933	2/4/67	S 1	—
Manor House	?	—	?	?	?	S 1	—
Manor House (RF)	M&H 6 App	—	23	1899	2/3/30	S 1	—
Manor House (RF)	M&H 16 App	—	25	2/3/30	2/1/55	S 1	—
Manor House GF	?	—	2	2/1/55	?	EGF	—
PRIORY YARD							
Priory West	M&H 4 App	—	24	1907	1914	S 4	8' 6", 20' 0" x 10' 6". Secondhand locking App
Priory East	M&H 4 App	—	35	1907	1914	S 4	8' 6", 25' 0" x 12' 0". Secondhand locking App
Dairycoates West	M&H 16 App	—	100	1914	1962	S 4	Originally referred to as Gypsyville
Dairycoates West (FS)	M&H 16 App	—	70	1962	10/6/84	S 4	Extensive relocking etc for opening of Hessle Road, new box.

SCARBOROUGH BRANCH

Victoria Crossing	?	—	?	?	1891	S 1	8' 6", 17' 6" x 9' 9"
Victoria Crossing (RF)	Rly Sig Co	—	20	1891	8/7/45	S 1	as above
Walton Street	M&H 6in App	2	9	1886	22/6/24	S 1	All wood construction 4' 6", 10' 6" x 8' 3"
Walton Street	M&H 16 App	2	27	22/6/24	—	S 4	—
Walton Street (FS)	M&H 16 App	—	20	—	31/3/80	S 4	Boom gates installed 1/12/63
Walton Street (FR)	—	—	—	31/3/80	19/4/87	S 4	Now a gate box
Walton St Gate box	—	—	—	19/4/87	16/7/89	—	Portakabin
Cottingham Jct	M&H App	—	14	1874	1899	S 1	8' 0", 15' 6" x 10' 0"
Cottingham Jct (RF)	Stevens 4 App	—	20	1899	4/1906	S 1	Line to Hessle Road made double
Cottingham Jct	M&H 16 App	—	35	4/1906	1927	S 1	Box extended and RF. Provision of "Radiator" sidings
Cottingham South	M&H 16 App	—	35	1927	17/8/72	S 1	Cottingham Jct renamed Cottingham South

MAIN LINE

Hessle Jct	S&F	—	14	1874	1904	?	8' 0", 13' 0" x 9' 9"
Hessle Haven	M&H 16 App	—	60	1912	—	S 4	—
Hessle Haven (FE)	M&H 16 App	—	65	—	—	S 4	Frame was re-locked and extended.
Hessle Haven (FS)	M&H 16 App	—	?	—	—	S 4	—
Hessle Haven (FS)	M&H 16 App	1	11	17/7/75	27/2/83	S 4	Provision of a gate wheel and mechanical barriers. Last new GW installation in the UK
Hessle Grange	?	?	?	?	?	?	—
Hessle New Jct	M&H 16 App	—	47	1904	—	—	—
Hessle New Jct (FE)	M&H 16 App	—	55	1907	—	—	8' 6", 29' 0" x 12' 0"
Hessle New Jct (FE)	M&H 16 App	—	65	1911	—	—	—
Hessle East	M&H 16 App	—	65	?	11/7/65	—	Hessle New Jct renamed, date unknown
Hessle Road Jct	S&F	1	?	pre1868	?	SSS	Very early application of a gate wheel
Hessle Road Jct	M&H 11 App	2	58	?	?	?	—
Hessle Road Jct (FE)	M&H 11 App	2	82	1899	?	?	—
Hessle Road Jct	M&H 16 App	2	109	?	7/10/62	S 4	Probably above box extended or part rebuilt
Hessle Road	WH NX panel	—	—	7/10/62	S.I.U.	BR	NE Region design box.
Chalk Lane GB	?	—	2	?	16/2/04	—	Wooden hut, later exposed GF 5' 6" x 5' 6".

MAIN LINE cont.

Chalk Lane GB	M&H 16 App	1	8	16/2/04	23/9/73	GB	Barriers installed 19/20 Aug 1972. Crossing now CCTV Hessle Rd. No control of signals from 7/10/62
St Georges Road GB	M&H 6 App	2	4	?	1904	?	At ground level, 8' 0" x 8' 0"
St Georges Road GB	?	1	7	1904	1940	GB	3' 0" x 11' 0" x 9' 6".
St Georges Road GB (RF)	?	1	—	1940	30/9/73	—	No control of signals from 7/10/62
Anlaby Road Jct	M&H 6 App	2	22	1875	—	S 1	8' 0", 20' 0" x 9' 6". Special splayed corners.
Anlaby Road Jct (RF)	M&H 16 App	2	22	?	?	S 1	Level crossing closed 31/7/64
West Parade	M&H 16 App	—	120	17/4/04	?	S 2	8' 6", 63' 0" x 14' 0".
West Parade (RL)	M&H 16 App	—	105	?	6/10/75	S 2	
West Parade (FS)	M&H 16 App	—	67	6/10/75	29/3/80	S 2	
Argyle Street LC	?	?	?	?	1887	?	Level crossing abolished
West Parade	S&F	—	32	1875	—	?	Special splayed corners. 7' 6", 21' 6" x 9' 9".
West Parade (FA)	S&F re-locked	—	30	?	17/4/04	?	
Park Street LC	?	?	?	?	?	S 1	20/12/1871 work starts on abolition of level crossing
Park Street	M&H App	—	46	1875	3/5/05	S 1	Special splayed corners. 8' 0", 26' 0" x 10' 0".
Park Street	M&H Type B	—	179	3/5/05	24/4/38	S 2	11' 6", 43' 0" x 12' 0".
Paragon Temporary	M&H 16 App	—	30	1904	3/5/05	?	
Paragon Yard	M&H App	—	33	1875	—	S 1	Special splayed corners. 10' 0", 24' 9" x 9' 9".
Paragon Yard (FE)	M&H App	—	34	—	1904		
Paragon	M&H Type B	—	143	1904	24/4/38	S 2	36' 0" x 12' 0"
Paragon	WH O.C.S.	—	—	24/4/38	—	LNE	LNER Type 13 box
Paragon (RP)	NX	—	—	2/12/84	S.I.U.	LNE	Extensive alterations to layout

N.E.R. RIVERSIDE QUAY BRANCH

Billingsgate	M&H 16 App	—	4+6k	11/5/07	1914	?	All timber construction 6' 0", 12' 0" x 10' 0".
Billingsgate (FE)	M&H 16 App	—	6+7k	1914	27/2/37	?	k = keys
Riverside Quay	M&H 16 App	—	10	11/5/07	1913	?	All timber construction 3' 0", 12' 0" x 10' 0".
Riverside Quay (FE)	M&H 16 App	—	20	1913	19/9/38	?	Box also extended
Riverside Quay	M&H 16 App	—	?	1946	?	?	Temporary signal box opened by LNER and built from recovered materials, for B.A.O.R. traffic

N.E.R. NEWINGTON BRANCH

Newington	M&H 11 App	1	12	1899	—	S 1	All timber construction 8' 6", 14' 0" x 10' 0".
Newington GB	M&H 11 App	1	12	—	1925	S 1	Reduced to gate box during Great War
Newington GB (RF)	M&H 16 App	2	14	1925	23/5/65	S 1	Provision of Tram crossing
Water Works	M&H 11 App	—	9	c1899	1906	?	All timber construction. B.o.T. report of Aug 1899 refers to existing temporary box
Water Works	M&H 16 App	2	7	1925	1932	S 4	Provision of level crossing for new road.
Water Works GB	M&H 16 App	2	7	1932	23/5/65	S 4	Reduced in status to Gate Box

VICTORIA DOCK BRANCH

Cemetery Jct	?	—	?	?	1881	?	—
Cemetery Gates	?	?	?	?	?	?	—
Cemetery Gates Jct	?	2	20	1881	—	S1	8' 6", 21' 0" x 9' 6"
Botanic Gardens	?	2	20	—	—	S1	CGJ renamed 1/11/1881
Botanic Gardens (RF)	?	2	39	1898	30/10/37	S1	Box extended now. 8' 6", 25' 0" x 12' 0"
Botanic Gardens (TFA)	?	—	4	8/10/00	2/10/37	S1	Dates refer to tram service
Botanic Gardens (RF)	M&H 16 App	2	31	31/10/37	1968	S1	—
Terry Street GB	M&H	2	5	?	—	GB	3' 0" x 9' 0" x 9' 0". Secondhand locking frame
Park Road GB	M&H	2	5	?	—	GB	Terry Street renamed
Park Road GB (RF)	M&H App	2	1	15/6/43	1968	—	No control of signals from 15/6/43
Stepney Station	?	?	?	?	?	?	—
Stepney Gates	M&H 11 App	2	18	?	?	?	—
Stepney	M&H 11 App	2	26	10/2/01	16/10/37	S1	22' x 12' x9'
Stepney (TFA)	M&H 1891	—	4	-/2/01	3/9/38		Dates refer to tram service
Stepney (RF)	M&H 16 App	2	21	17/10/37	1968	S1	—
Sculcoates Sidings	?	—	8	12/8/09?	1925	?	Not a Block Post
Sculcoates Goods	S&F Rocker	—	12	?	—	S 1	8' 6", 13' 9" x 8' 0".
Sculcoates Goods (FRL)	Tappet locking	—	—	-/10/06	—	S 1	—
Sculcoates Goods (RF)	?	—	15	6/9/08	1912	S 1	—
Sculcoates Stn/Bridge	S&F Rocker	1	14	?	?	S 1	8' 6", 14' 0" x 10' 0".
Sculcoates Stn/Bridge (RF)	M&H 6in App	1	14	?	1905	S 1	Secondhand locking frame ex Picton.
Sculcoates Station	M&H	1	?	1905	1907	—	Temporary box for construction period of new bridge.
Sculcoates	M&H 16 App	1	46	1907	—	S 4	B.o.T. inspection 6/8/1907. 8' 6", 28' 0" x 12' 0".
Wincolmlee (Sculcoates)	M&H 16 App	1	46	—	—	S 4	Called Wincolmlee in B.o.T report of 29/9/1910
Wincolmlee (FS)	M&H 16 App	1	31	—	1968	S 4	
Wilmington Bridge	M&H 16 App	—	5	10/5/07	S.I.U.	BB	Not a Block Post. Now property of Hull Corporation
Wilmington Jct	M&H 6in App	1	?	?	?	?	8' 0", 23' 0" x 10' 0".Interlocking installed 1879
Wilmington Jct	?	1	24	?	?	?	8' 6", 29' 0" x 12' 0". Provision of replacement box
Wilmington Jct	M&H 16 App	—	45	1912	13/6/13?	S 4	Provision of new station and junction
Wilmington Jct (FE)	M&H 16 App	—	50	13/6/13?	14/12/68	S 4	Provision of a 5 lever extension
New Goods Jct	?	—	?	?	?	?	NER records are indiscriminate
Wilmington Goods	?	—	?	?	—	—	New Goods Jct renamed. Closed half year end 6/04.
Dansom Lane	?	?	?	?	1904	?	Prior to 1904 was a level crossing only
Dansom Lane	M&H 4 App	1	31	1904	—	S 2	8' 6", 24' 0" x 12' 0". Secondhand locking frame.
Dansom Lane (RF)	?	1	36	?	14/12/68	S 2	New frame.
Southcoates	?	?	?	?	?	S 1	—
Southcoates (RF ?)	M&H App	2	30+2	?	?	S 1	9' 0", 23' 6" x 13' 6".

VICTORIA DOCK BRANCH cont							
Southcoates (TFA)	?	—	4	10/4/00	17/4/00	S 1	Tram frame added. Dates refer to tram service
Southcoates (RF)	M&H 16 App	2	31	1904	—	S1/S2	Box extended now 9' 0", 25' 6" x 20' 0".
Southcoates (RF)	M&H 16 App	2	34/40	?	1944	S1/S2	—
Southcoates (RF)	M&H 16 App	2	41	1944	14/12/68	S1/S2	—
Southcoates GF	M&H 6in App	—	3	?	?	EGF	Probably installed 1904
Southcoates Goods	?	?	?	?	—		Closed half year end 6/04
Hedon Road GB	?	1	11	?	1903	?	—
WITHERNSEA BRANCH							
Craven Street Crossing	?	?	10	?	—	?	Level crossing out 1893. Closed half year end 12/03.
Southcoates Lane GB	?	—	?	?	?	?	Level crossing out 25/2/1914
Hull Joint Dock Jct	M&H 4 App	—	25	1903	1919	S 1	8' 0", 20' 6" x 10' 3". Secondhand frame
Holderness Drain (RF)	M&H 16 App	—	30	—	—	S 1	HJDJ reframed and renamed. (see below)
Holderness Drain North	M&H 16 App	—	30	—	25/2/68	S 1	HD officially called Holderness Drain North, new frame ordered 25/8/20. Now no longer a junction with Withernsea branch, and worked timber plots only.
Marfleet	M&H App	—	7	?	12/1903	—	Wood cover
Marfleet	M&H 16 App	—	25	12/1903	28/10/68	S 2	8' 6", 18' 0" x 12' 0".
Marfleet Crossing GF	?	?	4	1912	12/2/34	?	Replaced by road bridge
DRYPOOL GOODS LINES							
Southcoates Lane	M&H App	—	55	?	c1938	S1/S4	Closed and re-opened on several occassions
Southcoates Lane GF	?	—	5	24/2/42	5/1/70	?	—
Hedon Branch GF	?	—	?	28/10/68	12/11/72	EGF	—
Sweet Dews GF	?	—	?	28/10/68	7/87	EGF	—
HORNSEA BRANCH							
Wilmington Inner Jct	M&H 6in App	—	11	1897	—	?	All timber construction 1' 0", 11' 6" x 10' 6".
Wilmington East	M&H 6in App	—	11	—	30/9/09	—	WIJ renamed
Wilmington East (FE)	M&H 6in App	—	12	30/9/09	1914	—	—
Garden Village GF	?	—	1	30/3/09	1914	EGF	Released from Wilmington East
Wilmington East	M&H 16 App	—	27	1914	2/1/60	S 4	Level crossing worked by hand
Hornsea Branch GF	?	—	?	28/10/68	12/11/72	?	—
Stoneferry Jct	M&H 16 App	—	25	1913	—	S 2	—
Stoneferry Jct	M&H 16 App	1	26	?	1/11/64	S 2	Provision of level crossing. Last new crossing in city
Sutton Road GB	M&H 6in App	—	5	11/06	1/11/64	?	—
Sutton	M&H App	—	6	?	1898	—	Timber hut on platform. 2' 6", 10' 0" x 8' 0".
Sutton	S&F App	—	21	1898	1964	S 1	—

Key:-
Makers: **E.O.D** - Evans O'Donnell; **LNE** - London & North Eastern Rly; **M&H** - Mackenzie & Holland; **NER** - North Eastern Rly; **Rly Sig Co**. - Railway Signalling Company; **S&F** - Saxby & Farmer; **WH** - Westinghouse.
Terms: **BB** - Bridge Box; **CCTV** - Closed circuit television; **CGF** - Covered Ground Frame; **EGF** - Exposed Ground Frame; **FA** - Frame altered; **FE** - Frame extended; **FR** - Frame removed; **FRL** - Frame re-locked; **FS** - Frame shortened; **GB** - Gate Box; **GF** - Ground Frame; **LC** - Level Crossing; **LVRS** - Levers; **O.O.U.** - Out of use; **Reb** - Rebuilt; **RF** - Re-framed; **RL** - Re-locked; **RP** - Replacement Panel; **S.I.U.** - Still in use; **Spec** - Special; **SSS** - Saxby Signal Stage; **TFA** - Tram Frame added.

Note:- *Such is the contraction of Hull's railway system, there are now only two signalmen on duty within the city at any one time.*

For the opening of the railway the H&BR provided this signal box at Sculcoates and established a large goods yard. The yard, apart from dealing with general merchandise, was soon to accommodate several local coal merchants. On the Down side of the railway was the Bankside works of the British Gas Light & Coke Co. Ltd, this too was rail connected, as was the Hull Corporation Electricity Dept. Both continued to be rail served up to recent times, and the demise of the connections was only brought about by the rationalisation of their respective industries; mainly central electricity generating, and natural gas from the North Sea. The domestic coal sales fared a little better, and the remnants of the yard continued to be used for these purposes until the early 1990s. Sculcoates signal box was closed on Saturday 4th May 1968, and at that time contained a frame of 30 levers, this having replaced the original of 29 levers on 4th October 1954. After the demise of Sculcoates box, control of the new colour light signals and the remaining points which were now motor worked, became the responsibility of the Hessle Road power box signalman.
Authors Collection.

Dairycoates West from 5A bridge. We are looking east at the rearranged junction completed in November 1935 for the opening of the new Inwards Yard the following month. The lines are left to right - Down Main North; Up North Main; Down South Main and Up South Main, all of which led to Dairycoates East some 848 yards further on. Those lines running across the picture are the Up and Down goods lines from Hessle Road to St Andrews Dock Junction; these being 872 yards and 600 yards respectively from Dairycoates West signal box. Former NER lower quadrant signals predominate with not one upper quadrant signal to be seen. On the far left is the Dairycoates engine shed coaling plant and to the right of that the shed itself. In the nape of the junction, standing on their own siding are P.Way staff vehicles consisting of a Great Western open wagon in use as a rubbish skip, a six wheel exNER carriage with another similar vehicle beyond. To the right of the main line is Outward Yard whilst beyond are the fish processing factories and docks, complete with trawlers, on the slipways of the St Andrew's Dock extension. *Authors collection.*

Some twenty seven years later than the previous picture is this almost similar view of Dairycoates West on the 8th August 1962. The main line track layout has been simplified, gone are the Up and Down South Main lines from Dairycoates East and the remodelled junction, brought about by the opening of the new Hessle Road power signal box, is virtually as it was before the 1935 alterations. The coaling plant is still doing business and the engine shed has itself been remodelled, the roundhouse nearest to the camera now no longer in being though the turntable still functions for outside stabling of locomotives. The remaining engine sheds have been rebuilt to a standard period design. On the P.Way siding the accomodation vehicles have been swapped for some less ancient bogie carriages but otherwise the scene is much the same. *Ken Hoole.*

As part of the conversion of the Hornsea branch to double line it was necessary during 1898 to provide a new signal box at Sutton. Containing a locking frame of 21 levers, and unusually for the period of Saxby & Farmer manufacture, it almost certainly would have been assembled from recovered material. Originally 17 levers were in use, but by the time of the picture (10th October 1964) owing to the removal of certain signals, and the trailing Mains crossover at the west end of the station only 9 levers remained in use. The signal box was built to the contemporary S1 design, but for some reason is equipped with non-standard oblong shaped locking room windows, normally these would be arched shaped. Regretfully there is no record of the inside dimensions of the signal box, but its predecessor was of all wood construction, and located on the platform, 2ft 6ins above rail height, with inside dimensions of 10ft x 8ft, and it contained a McKenzie & Holland locking frame of 6 levers, of which 5 were in use.

by arrangement with Ian Scotney.

To work all the new and altered connections at West Parade the NER provided a replacement signal box immediately to the west of the Argyle Street bridge. For some reason, even though the new installation was approximately a quarter of a mile away from the street of that name, the original signal box title of West Parade was retained. The replacement which was built between the Main and Scarborough lines had the lever frame overlooking the branch lines and engine shed, so technically all main line trains passed behind the box. When first opened a locking frame of 120 levers was provided, and this, to permit the signalmen access to the front look out balcony, was divided into two equal halves, the frame sections being levers numbers 1 to 60 and 61 to 120. The look out balcony is quite prominent in this view of Sunday 4th June 1978. Owing to the length of the box access steps were provided at each end, and to permit the signalmen a good view of main line trains the rear of the box, apart from the chimney stacks, was fully glazed. In the background can be seen the one time fear of all the lower classes, "The Work House", or to use the correct and proper title "The Anlaby Road Poor Law Institution". This place eventually became the Western General Hospital and then later still, Hull Royal Infirmary. "The Workhouse" had figured prominently in the well known accident of Monday 14th February 1927 when, to expedite the swift removal of the dead and injured, the boundary wall was breached. West Parade signal box passed into history less then two years after this view was captured when at 23.20hrs on Saturday 29th March 1980 signalman Peter Burke closed the box for good. *Authors collection.*

The early history of Graving Dock signal box is a little confusing, and when one looks back into the minutes of the H&BR one finds reference to a signal box called Alexandra Dock East. We do not know with any certainty when this box was first brought into use, except that by 1904 it features in the Company's records. Certainly no signal box called Alexandra Dock East ever appeared in any appendix circulated to the 'Servants of the Company', and therefore one can now only presume it was in use as a 'ground frame'. We conclude that owing to the anticipated increase in traffic which would be brought about by the opening of the new Joint Dock in 1914 it was necessary to convert the existing building into a Block Post. However, a new frame of 40 levers, and of the usual Evans O'Donnell 'Catch Handle' pattern was supplied by the Saxby Signal Co., and this is known to have been ready 1st April 1915. Owing to labour shortage, and effects of the Great War the new works were not brought into use until 10 a.m. 1st November 1920. The signal box was abandoned at 5.30 p.m. on Saturday 27th July 1968. *by arrangement with Ian Scotney.*

Unfortunately we are unable to give an exact date to this obviously posed interior view of West Parade signal box. Study of the lever frame tells one the date is later than 25th July 1954, but before the post 1957 provision of motor worked points, whilst the wall clock shows the time to be 8.55 p.m. Signalman Jackson rests on No.48 lever (Facing Point Lock to No.49 Up Scarborough to "D" Line Points), and to his left stands signalman Fred Rounding, whilst in the background the booking lad looks on from his desk. Both the signalmen continued in railway service until their eventual retirement some years later, but despite enquires made with contemporary railwaymen we have been unable to establish either the booking lad's name or his eventual fate. With the gradual decline in traffic the services of the lad were no longer required, and his post was eventually dispensed with. Then as traffic yet further declined the duties of the signalmen were again reduced, and by the time the box closed only one signalman per shift was called for. Apart from a few detail differences and the inevitable provision of more spare levers, when the box closed some 20 or more years later the interior had changed very little. *by arrangement N. Fleetwood.*

Paragon signal box 21st July 1973. To house the new panel and associated equipment in 1938 the LNER built this rather handsome signalbox which is a typical product of the 30s. Despite bomb damage in the last war the box continues to this day to serve the railway, and no doubt will do so for many years to come. The concrete erection on the right is the surviving air raid shelter. *M.A.King.*

When first opened in April 1938 the new Paragon box was at the forefront of technology, but one must admit that by Sunday 28th October 1979 when at 11.11 hrs relief signalman Bill Vickers posed for this photograph the equipment was looking a little dated. By this time the outside layout had been somewhat rationalised from the original, and conspicuous by their absence are "North Sidings", "A" Line, and "F" Line, however apart from the night and Sunday shifts, there was still enough activity to keep two signalmen busy. Despite the dated appearance of the panel, it must be remembered that this, and a handful of other pre-war installations led the way towards today's "High-tech" panel boxes. Although track circuits were provided throughout, traditional block working was retained until 2nd December 1984 when this panel was replaced in conjunction with extensive alterations. *Authors coll..*

This view like several others in this volume was taken from the RCTS excursion of October 1964. The train is passing Dairycoates East signal box on the Up Main Goods and heading westward. When first opened in late 1906 the signal box, then called Dairycoates Junction, had an interlocking frame of only 90 levers which by 1914 had been increased to 100, and later still a further 45 were added. Post 1925 it was necessary to add one more lever, bringing the total to 146, thus making Dairycoates East by far the largest mechanical signal box in the city. By the time of our picture the Facing Point Locks had been removed, and the signalling was therefore no longer up to passenger line standards. It was necessary to clamp all the facing points over which the train passed, and the railway officials seen by the lineside will have been busily engaged on this duty. In similar vein, to allow a passenger train to run on a "Permissive Block" goods only line, it is first compulsory to convert the block working to "Absolute", and here the signalman is seen going back to his box after giving the driver the "Block Conversion Ticket". *Ian K.Watson.*

It was as late as 1886 before a proper level crossing was provided at Walton Street, and due to the acute angle of the road/rail crossing the span of the gates was a massive 55 feet. The larger of the two gates was 41 feet in length, whilst the smaller of the pair a mere 14 feet; even the wicket gates were quite a respectable 8 feet long. The signal box which is so well illustrated in this fine Edwardian view looks a little out of place and very much an afterthought, forced upon the front garden of No.1 Railway Cottages. There can have been little room inside, for in an area of only 10ft 6ins x 8ft 3ins was crammed two gate wheels, a frame of 9 levers, plus a stove, booking desk, and all the other equipment of a working signal box. During the final months of 1890, or possibly early in the following year, work was found for all the spare levers when the connections to the nearby carriage sidings and sheds were put in. Although basically of the standard 'S1' design of the period, the signal box is rather unusually of timber construction. After a life of 38 years this particular signal box became redundant and was replaced when the construction of the junction to the ex H&BR system necessitated a larger box. By today's standards the two oil lamps are quite largely proportioned, the observant will note that the gate lamp is fitted with red coloured glasses. Prominent on the front of the signal box is the Signal Department fault board, this was coloured white on the obverse and red on the reverse side. Prior to mass communication this was often the only means the signalman had to inform the signal fitter or lineman if the signal box equipment was functioning or not. The use of these boards on the NER, if not nationally, was dispensed with during the later part of 1922. In the background can be seen an advert telling all, and pointing any interested party in the direction of the works of G & A Leake monumental stone masons. Right up to the early 1960s Messrs Leake and Co. traded from premises on Springbank West, and older readers will well remember their famous statue of King Edward VII. This incidentally remained in their former yard long after they had ceased trading, and today survives as the property of a local auctioneer. The telegraph pole just outside the railway boundary is the property of the Hull Corporation Telephone Dept. Its single line arm indicates there is as yet little local demand for Graham Bell's invention, but if nothing else the three insulators suggest at least that number of subscribers in the immediate vicinity. Apart from the removal of the mechanically worked gates as long ago as 1st December 1963, at a casual glance the scene today is not all that changed. The railway cottages are no longer in use for domestic purposes and now form the offices of Ced Francis, a local car dealer. *Memory Lane Hull.*

Holderness Drain signal box as it was first called was one of the last signal boxes to be constructed by the H&BR and was more or less contemporary with the installations at both Bridges Junction, and Liverpool Street. All three of these signal boxes had their origins in the Joint Dock agreement, but regretfully no photographic record is known of either Bridges Junction or Liverpool Street. Coincidentally all of these boxes were located on embankments and were therefore of all wood construction and supported on timber piles. Holderness Drain South as it was soon renamed by the LNER had by far the longest life of the trio, almost 60 years, but this finally came to an end during December 1973. *reproduced by arrangement with Nick Fleetwood.*

As the name suggests, Hull Joint Dock Junction was purpose built to give rail access during the construction period of the new dock. At the same time that part of the Withernsea branch was made into a double line, but the new railway to the dock was only single track. According to the surviving records of the NER, the interlocking frame which was second-hand and of 25 levers, was installed in the new signal box during March 1903. The exact date when the new works were brought into use is now lost, but it remains on record the BoT inspected them on 11th December 1903. At first there was only the junction to the dock, in April 1904 a trailing mains crossover was added, then either in late 1910 or early 1911 a temporary Down siding was brought into use, this being inspected by the BoT in February 1911. The Down line is the one to Withernsea (nearest the camera), the difference between the original and the new bridge girders is also evident. With the eventual diversion of the Withernsea branch, Joint Dock Junction was no longer required, and a NER minute No.20856 of 10th April 1919 reads, " Resolved extra expenditure of £64/-/9d including closure and removal of Joint Dock Junction Box". Although closed the signalbox was not removed, and was eventually fitted with a new interlocking frame and brought back into use. It was then renamed Holderness Drain, and later still to save confusion with the not far away ex H&BR box Holderness Drain North. To serve the various timber stacking grounds that were eventually established in the area Holderness Drain North remained in use until February 1968. *Memory Lane, Hull.*

Virtually nothing is known of the original gate box at St George's Road level crossing apart from it having four levers and two gate wheels. A new box, featured here in the late 1960s, containing an interlocking frame of seven levers and one gate wheel was provided sometime during 1904. This box became redundant on Sunday 30th September 1973. Rather interestingly in the mid 1960s Hull Corporation formulated a plan to close off the road and completely abandon the crossing and like so many other similar schemes came to nothing and was soon forgotten. Today the crossing is still with us because on Sunday 3rd December 1972 modern lifting barriers were installed, now remotely controlled with the aid of closed circuit television from Hessle Road signal box. *L.Carr.*

(above) **The ground frame at Hump Top, 19th June 1963, east end of Outward Yard, seen after the cabin surrounding it had gone up in flames, converting it into an open-air one. Someone has rigged up a makeshift windbreak on the west side. No.15 pilot is disappearing down into the yard probably to right a wrong shunt.** *Peter Rose.*

(opposite) **West Parade came into being during 1848 when the main line trains from Selby and the branch trains from Bridlington were diverted into the new Paragon station and converged at this point. On 1st July 1864 the Hornsea and Withernsea branch trains were also diverted to Paragon and West Parade was firmly established on the local railway map. By late 1875 a signal box fitted with a properly interlocked frame of 32 levers was in use. With the rebuilding of Paragon station, and the opening of Botanic Gardens engine shed, West Parade junction took on even more significance. There was now a total of seven running lines into and out of Paragon and these, rather unusually, were identified by letter rather than name. In the Down direction were A, B, D and F lines; in the Up direction C, E and G. The most prominent feature of the new layout was the "Double Scissors" crossover, placed between B, C, D and E lines. This new layout was brought into use in stages between 17th April 1904 and the early months of 1905. Apart from the introduction of colour light signals to replace the semaphores, the layout was destined to remain unchanged until the early 1970s. Reproduced here is a fine view ,taken from Argyle Street bridge, of 61437 a B16/2 heading for Bridlington with a parcels train in late 1961. To the left of the locomotive is the new carriage washing plant built on the site of "A" line.** *Neville Stead*

(right) **On Saturday 10th October 1964 the Railway Correspondence & Travel Society organised a tour covering most of the railway lines in Hull. The special is seen here on the Down Newington branch heading north to Cottingham South Junction, and about to pass over Waterworks level crossing. This crossing along with its controlling signal box was provided in the early months of 1925 at the expense of the Hull Corporation. For the first seven years of its life Waterworks was a 'Block Post', but from 1932 was reduced in status to a Gate box remaining as such until the line was abandoned in May 1965.** *I K Watson.*

(above) **The eastern vista from Wilmington Junction signal box in 1955 with a three coach train approaching on the Up Hornsea line. The unidentified motive power is one of the ex LMS Fowler 2-6-2 tank engines allocated to Botanic Gardens at this period. The track over the down line bridge span has been re-laid with flat bottom rails, and the lack of a lock bar to the facing point lock indicates that a track circuit has been installed. The up main span still carries the traditional chaired bullhead rails. Prior to 1910, this junction was the site of one of the city's numerous level crossings. Over to the right are the Up and Down goods lines from Dansom Lane (688 yards eastwards) whilst beyond the goods lines, at ground level, is Wilmington goods yard.** *The late Dick Leadham.*

(opposite top) **Seen from the window of Wilmington Junction signal box, circa 1955, J73 No.68363 shunts what appears to be a train of empty mineral wagons probably from the nearby Earle's cement works. The houses in the left background are those of the terraces off Withernsea Street, whilst the ones running parallel to the railway are appropriately named Earles Row.** *The late Dick Leadham.*

(opposite bottom) **Wilmington station as viewed from Wilmington Junction signal box circa 1955. Nearest the camera is the Down Main (the Hornsea and Withernsea line). Shown to advantage is the island platform of the 1912 built station, the main entrance of which was at a lower level on Foster Street and unlike everything else in the picture still exists in 1995. The signals are a mix of NER originals and BR whilst the point rodding is the original round pattern type. The two 'blank runs' in the centre of the rodding run came about when Track Circuits were installed on the main lines and the rodding which worked the Fouling Bars was no longer required and removed.** *The late Dick Leadham.*

THOSE LEVEL CROSSINGS AGAIN

The horse still reigned supreme when this Edwardian view of Stepney level crossing was taken. Although the electric tramway was established, the internal combustion engine still had to make its impact on society and here four different modes of horse-drawn transport await the passage of a NER 0-6-2T heading bunker first towards Victoria Dock. Just above the enclosed gentlemen's carriage, second from left, can be seen one of the special tram signals as described elsewhere in this volume. On the roadway, connecting the "In and Out" tram lines, is a trailing crossover. *Memory Lane, Hull.*

Sixty years ago motorists were as impatient as they are today as evidenced by this unusual scene at Stepney level crossing on Wednesday 27th May 1936. Captured on film by gateman Fisher, whose original print is endorsed 12.56 p.m. At first sight the incident depicted appears to be technically impossible but due to normal wear and tear in the rodding connections of the gate mechanism it was possible for the gates to spring past the motor lorry albeit with a little damage. The lorry, belonging to a firm of Leeds coopers, was trapped for 15 minutes according to a contemporary report in the Hull Daily Mail and, although there was no personal injury, the signalman did have the gate wheel knocked out of his hand with the impact. As one would expect even a short closure such as this could cause traffic chaos and diversions were set up along nearby Cave Street and Terry Street; notice the motor bus in the background attempting a multi-point turn to escape the hold-up. The trams of course had no option but to stand and await the outcome. A few weeks after the incident the driver of the ensnared lorry had to answer to the local magistrates. *C.Fisher/Memory Lane, Hull.*

(opposite bottom) This view captured in the final years of Victoria's reign is the only known record of the Hedon Road level crossing. Work has commenced on the construction of the new road in readiness for the replacement road bridge and the eventual abandonment of the level crossing. The houses visible behind the railway cottage are those in Seward Street, and probably the left hand chimney belongs to a sugar mill in nearby Williamson Street, whilst the one in the right background is the property of a Bellamy Street saw mill. *Memory Lane, Hull.*

(above) This cameraman was on the north side of Spring Bank and looking across the railway towards the west, when he composed this very typical mid 1960s view. Forming part of the backdrop is almost all of the late Norman Duggleby's toy and cycle shop, this in its self was for more than three decades a local institution. Be it a pram, a gents or ladies bike or one for a child full size or small they would have it. There is also a good chance that many of the "40 something born again trainspotters", presently reading this tome will have had their first train set bought from this same shop. Rather surprisingly, and despite appearance, these shops, which stand on the site of the main gates and lodge of the one time "The Hull General Cemetery Co." were not built until the late 1920s. Beyond can be seen part of the cemetery which at that time was still open for business, and the occasional interment. It was due to the close proximity of these burial grounds that the station took its original name of Cemetery, the suffix "Gates" not being added until later. The level crossing seen here is not the original, but an enlarged version put in during the summer of 1900 to cater for the coming of the electric tram cars, which after some delay eventually crossed the railway as from Monday 8th October 1900. The enlarged and replacement gates increased the road width to 38ft 6ins, whilst the four wicket gates provided for a footpath or pavement of 8ft 6ins in width. Opposite the signal box is the now redundant gateman's hut. This became surplus to requirements a year or two after the withdrawal of the Hornsea and Withernsea branch passenger trains, when the powers-that-be decreed the services of an additional man were no longer justified. The sole duty of the gate or flagman, as he was often called, had been to assist the signalman in closing the gates, but this apparently humble task was performed by some better than others. On being summoned from his hut by the signalmans bell, the gateman walked out onto the road and proudly displayed his intimidating red flag, holding it so that road traffic would stop. At the same time he would further assist the signalman with the gates, by pulling on a short length of conveniently attached chain. Some became quite adept at their task, whilst others soon learned the technically impossible art of how to pull a gate with a slack chain. Even in those now far off and halcyon days, motorists, like their present day counterparts, despised delay and paid little respect to either the gateman or his red flag. It will therefore be of little surprise to learn that at least one irate "Servant of the Company" hurled his red flag "javelin" style through the front windscreen of an oncoming Corporation bus. Regretfully, though the tale is well known within local railway folk lore, for some reason the outcome of the incident remains unrecorded. After the departure of the resident flagman, when he required to close the gates it became the practice of the signalman to summon the help of the local constabulary. As older readers will well remember prior to the provision of the present day road traffic lights there was for many years a policeman, and then later a traffic warden on point duty here. Just as before the signalman continued to ring his bell, but now on hearing its sound the policeman or warden obligingly stopped all road traffic, and thus enabled the signalman to close the gates with ease. There was of a course a price to be paid for this unofficial service - cups of tea in the signal box. *I.K.Watson.*

GOODS TRAINS, GOODS LINES AND YARDS

Within two months of this view being taken, steam traction, apart from a handful of Saturday only holiday trains which mainly passed straight through the city, was as good as finished. Seen here heading westwards and passing the 1910 built Alexandra Dock signal box on Thursday 20th April 1967 is WD 2-8-0 90695. Although not apparent, the train is made up entirely of loaded tank wagons from the Saltend oil refinery. 90695 had first come to Dairycoates as early as March 1949. With the demise of steam working the engine was transferred away to West Hartlepool from where it was finally withdrawn three months later. *The Rev. David Benson.*

A long train of empty open wagons is moved past Dairycoates shed towards Dairycoates East Junction by 4MT 43079 in mid-November 1963. *Peter Rose.*

In this circa 1910 view of Southcoates, from the Hull & Barnsley Railway overbridge just north of Alexandra Dock we look towards the east. To the middle left are the earth works for the new railway which eventually permitted through running between the H&BR at Bridges Junction, and the NER at Southcoates Lane. In the foreground, and in hopeful anticipation of the extra traffic the new "Joint Dock" will generate, a gang of platelayers are busy laying in the point work for the new and altered Sweet Dews sidings. Incidentally although not visible here, the name of the sidings was taken from a farm in nearby Newbridge Road, and where in 1938 the author sited one of the Air Raid Wardens' Posts for which he was then responsible. The goods train which is passing the Southcoates Outer Home signal is on the Up Withernsea line and appears to consist mainly of empty wagons. *Memory Lane Hull.*

With a well coaled tender an indication the engine is not long "off shed" Class B16/3 No.61467 is heading west through Botanic towards Anlaby Road with a goods working from Dansom Lane. After being condemned in June 1964, 61467 like eight of its sisters was sold to Draper scrap metal dealers who would eventually commence cutting her up for scrap at their Sculcoates yard on Monday 26th October 1964. *I.K.Watson.*

A busy period at Hessle Haven on 16th July 1964. WD 90351 on J06 pilot (Wilmington - Hessle Quarry chalk empties) travels west on the Up Main whilst behind the signal box another WD waits for the same road with mineral empties for the West Riding. In the distance 90092 makes its way towards Loaded Mineral Yard with a heavy coal train. Hessle Haven formed the western boundary of the Hull West Yard area - a fact which today would be hard to believe. *Peter Rose.*

Outward Yard in August 1963 with a 350 h.p. Class 12 diesel shunter working the west end shunting pilot turn. B16/3 no.61467 sets out for Sheffield with the 7.20 p.m. SO mixed freight. The decades since this Saturday evening scene was captured have not been kind to Hull's railway system, none of these yards remain and the railway no longer handles the vast tonnages of freight which once passed through them. *Peter Rose.*

61032 STEMBOK takes the route from Springbank West to Springbank South on the 18th September 1964, with a train of empty coal wagons from Calvert Lane to Empty Mineral Yard. The bridge, which has not seen a train since the late 1980's is still in situ today. *Peter Rose.*

I make no excuse for once more featuring 90695, this time passing the closed Botanic Gardens station early in 1967. The train is made up entirely of tank wagons and the lack of "Cover or Barrier Wagons" between the tender and train tells one the tanks are conveying anything but petrol. Like in the other views a shuntstick remains wedged through the front framing of the locomotive, but this time, to ring the changes, the local trip number is now J01. About this period several of the local coal merchants were still operating from Botanic, but despite this there does not appear to be any wagons in the yard. The coal yard was destined to outlive the railway by many years, and the last merchant who by then was only trading on a part time basis did not finally vacate the site until the summer of 1994.

Authors collection.

HULL FREIGHT TRAIN DEPARTURES (11th July to 25th September 1927)

Class	Day(s) Run	Destination	Hull Mineral dep.	Hull Goods dep.	Hull other Location	depart.
B Goods	MX	Doncaster Decoy		12.10 am		
B Goods	MX	Leeds Neville Hill			Priory Yard	12.20 am
B Goods	MFX	York via Gascoigne Wood		12.40 am		
B Goods	MX	Barnsley			Priory Yard	12.45 am
B Mineral	MX(Q)	Barnsley Pinder Oaks	1.00 am			
B Mineral	MX(Q)	Brodsworth	1.10 am (note a)			
B Goods LMS	MX	Goole Potters Grange		1.10 am		
B Goods	MX	York Holgate Sidings via Gascoigne Wood			Priory Yard	1.15 am
B Goods	MX	Normanton		1.45 am		
B Goods	MX	Lincoln Holmes			Priory Yard	1.55 am
B Empties	MX	Doncaster Decoy	2.15 am			
B Goods	MX	Ardsley			Priory Yard	2.25 am
B Mineral	MX(Q)	Bullcroft Colliery	2.45 am (note b)			
B Goods	MX	Doncaster Decoy			Priory Yard	3.00 am
B Goods		Normanton			Priory Yard	3.20 am
B Goods	MX(Q)	Hessle Road Junction			Drypool	3.25 am
B Mineral	MX(Q)	Annesley	3.30 am			
B Cattle Empties	MO	Bridlington		3.35 am		
B Mineral		Wath	3.45 am			
B Goods		Doncaster Decoy		3.50 am		
D Cattle Empties	MO	Withernsea		3.55 am		
A Goods		Scarborough Gallows Close		4.00 am		
D Gds & C/e	MO	Hornsea Bridge		4.10 am		
B Goods	TO	Bridlington		4.15 am		
B Mineral	(Q)	Dinnington	4.20 am			
B Goods	MO (Q)	Leeds Neville Hill		4.25 am		
B Goods	TX	Bridlington		4.30 am		
B Goods	MX	Colwick			Priory Yard	4.35 am
B Mineral		Normanton			Hessle Haven Sidings	5.00 am
B Cattle Empties	MO	South Howden			Springhead	5.14 am
B Mineral		Hexthorpe	5.20 am			
D Goods		Withernsea		5.40 am		
B Mineral	(Q)	Silverwood Sidings	5.55 am			
B Mineral	(Q)	Stainforth & Hatfield	6.10 am			
B Goods	(Q)	Normanton		6.25 am		
B Mineral	(Q)	Bullcroft Colliery	6.25 am (note c)			
B Mineral	(Q)	Firbeck Colliery	6.25 am (note d)			
A Goods		Withernsea		6.25 am		
B Mineral		Gascoigne Wood			Hessle Haven Sidings	6.35 am
B Mineral	(Q)	Warmsworth	6.35			
B Goods		Driffield		6.40 am		
D Goods		Thorne North		6.45 am		
B Goods		Market Weighton		6.55 am		
A Goods		Hornsea Bridge		7.00 am		
B Mineral		Bullcroft Junction			Springhead	7.00 am
B Mineral	(Q)	Hickleton Colliery			Sculcoates	7.05 am
B Mineral	(Q)	Denaby	7.20 am			
D Goods	MX	Hornsea Bridge		7.45 am		
B Goods		Cudworth			Springhead	8.00 am
B Mineral	SO	Hessle Quarry			Wilmington	8.15 am
B Mineral	(Q)	Brodsworth	8.15 am			
B Mineral	(Q)	Firbeck Colliery	8.25 am			
B Goods	(Q)	York via Beverley		8.25 am		
D Goods		South Howden			Neptune Street	8.30 am
D Goods	SX	Bridlington		8.40 am		
D Goods		Wallingfen			Springhead	8.55 am
B Goods		Hensall Junction			Springhead	9.05 am
B Mineral	(Q)	Bullcroft Junction			Alexandra Dock	9.20 am
B Goods		Doncaster Decoy		9.20 am		
B Goods	MX(Q)	York via Gascoigne Wood		9.30 am		
B Mineral	MO(Q)	Milford Junction			Hessle Haven Sidings	9.35 am
D Goods		Brough		9.45 am		
B Goods		Cudworth			Springhead	9.50 am
B Mineral	SX	Hessle Quarry			Wilmington (note e)	9.55 am
B Mineral emp.	MX(Q)	Warsop	10.05 am			
B Mineral		Dinnington	10.20 am			
B Mineral	(note f)	Gascoigne Wood			Hessle Haven Sidings	10.30 am
B Goods		Hemsworth Sidings			Springhead	10.30 am
D Goods		Beverley		10.55 am		
B Mineral	(Q)	Staveley Town	10.55 am			
A Cattle	TO(Q)	Driffield		11.00 am		
B Goods LMS	MO(Q)	Goole LMS Junction			Priory Yard	11.09 am
B MIneral		Normanton			Hessle Haven Sidings	11.20 am
B Goods		Cudworth			Springhead	11.35 am
B Goods		Selby		11.50 am		
B Mineral	(Q)	Hickleton Colliery Junction	11.57 am			

B Mineral	SO	Hessle Quarry			Wilmington	12.05 pm
B Mineral	(Q)	Thurcroft	12.10 pm			
B Mineral	(Q)	Dinnington Colliery	12.20 pm			
B Mineral	(Q)	Rockingham	12.30 pm			
B Empties		Doncaster Decoy	12.45 pm			
B Mineral	SX	Hessle Quarry			Wilmington	12.55 pm
B Goods	SX FO(Q)	Leeds Neville Hill		1.05 pm		
No.1 Braked Fish	SX	Doncaster Decoy		1.15 pm		
B Goods	(Q)	Hexthorpe Top Yard		1.20 pm		
B Mineral	(Q)	Wharncliffe Silkstone	1.38 pm			
No.1 Braked Fish	SO(Q)	Doncaster Decoy		1.45 pm		
B Mineral	(Q)	Bullcroft Colliery	2.00 pm			
B Goods		Cudworth			Springhead	2.00 pm
B Mineral	(Q)	Orgreaves	2.10 pm			
No.1 Braked Fish	SO(Q)	Doncaster Decoy		2.20 pm		
No.1 Braked Fish	SX	Doncaster Decoy		3.00 pm		
C Mineral	(Q)	Hexthorpe	3.00 pm			
B Goods		Melton Sidings		3.05 pm		
B Mineral	(Q)	Stainforth & Hatfield	3.15 pm			
B Mineral		Wath	3.30 pm			
B Mineral	(Q)	Markham Main	3.45 pm			
B Goods		Cudworth			Springhead	3.45 pm
B Mineral	(Q)	Maltby	4.05 pm			
B Goods LMS		Goole LMS Junction		4.20 pm		
B Mineral	(Q)	Bullcroft Junction			Alexandra Dock	5.15 pm
A Fish	SO	Leeds Neville Hill		5.20 pm		
No.1 Braked Fish	SX	Doncaster Decoy		5.30 pm		
No.1 Braked Fish	SX(Q)	Doncaster Decoy		5.35 pm		
B Goods	SO	Doncaster Decoy		5.40 pm		
A Fish		York via Beverley		6.00 pm		
B Cattle	MO	York via Beverley		6.10 pm		
A Fish	SX	Leeds Neville Hill		6.15 pm		
B Goods		Hensall Junction			Springhead	6.35 pm
A Fish	SX	Normanton		6.40 pm		
B Fish	SO	Normanton		6.50 pm		
B Goods	SX	Doncaster Decoy		7.15 pm		
B Goods		Cudworth			Springhead	7.15 pm
B Goods LMS	SO	Wakefield		7.30 pm		
A Goods	SO	Woodford		7.45 pm		
B Goods LMS	SX	Bolton		7.45 pm		
B Goods	SO	Doncaster Central			Priory Yard	8.00 pm
B Goods		York via Gascoigne Wood			Priory Yard	8.20 pm
B Mineral	SO(Q)	Denaby	8.30 pm			
B Goods		York via Beverley		8.30 pm		
B Goods	SX	Normanton		8.35 pm		
A Goods		Ardwick		8.45 pm		
B Mineral	(Q)	Worksop	8.52 pm			
B Goods	SO	Leeds Neville Hill		8.55 pm		
A Goods	MWThO*	York via Beverley		9.00 pm		
A Goods	SO	Doncaster Decoy		9.05 pm		
A Goods	SX	Ardwick		9.10 pm		
B Goods	SO	Milford Junction		9.15 pm		
B Goods LMS	SX	Bradford		9.30 pm		
B Goods	SO(Q)	Normanton		9.40 pm		
B Mineral	SX	Gascoigne Wood			Hessle Haven Sidings	9.40 pm
A Goods	SX	Doncaster Decoy		9.45 pm		
A Goods	SX	Banbury Junction		10.00 pm		
B Mineral	(Q)	Broughton Lane	10.10 pm			
B Goods	SX	Leeds Neville Hill		10.10 pm		
B Goods LMS	SO	Goole LMS Junction		10.30 pm		
B Goods	SX	Bradford Goods		10.35 pm		
B Goods		Guide Bridge			Priory Yard	10.45 pm
B Mineral	SX	Normanton			Hessle Haven Sidings	10.52 pm
B Goods		Colwick		11.05 pm		
B Goods	SO	Sheffield		11.15 pm		
A Goods	SX	Monkwearmouth via Gas. W.		11.20 pm		
B Mineral	SX	Gascoigne Wood			Hessle Haven Sidings	11.20 pm
B Mineral	SX	Denaby	11.30 pm			
B Goods	ThO	York via Gascoigne Wood		11.43 pm		
B Goods	SX	Sheffield		11.50 pm		
B Goods	SO	Doncaster Decoy		11.55 pm		

SUNDAYS

B Goods		Ardsley	12.30 am			
B Goods		York via Gascoigne Wood		12.40 am		

Notes:

a. Runs alternately with 2.45 am Bullcroft Colliery. b. Runs alternately with 1.10 am Brodsworth. c. Runs alternately with d.

d. Runs alternately with c. e. Stoneferry departure 9.25 am (Q). f. Runs in path of 9.35 am Milford Junction MO(Q).

Q. Runs if required. * TFO is (Q).

HULL FREIGHT TRAIN DEPARTURES (30th June to 14th September 1952)

Class	Day(s) Run	Destination	Hull Mineral dep.	Hull Goods dep.	Hull other Location	depart
H	MX(Q)	Rotherham & Masboro	12.55 am			
H	MX	Selby Staggs Sidings		1.00 am		
H	MX	Croft Jct via Gascoigne W.		1.20 am		
H	MX	Lincoln Holmes		1.35 am		
H	MX	Stainforth & Hatfield		1.50 am		
H		Gascoigne Wood		3.30 am		
F		Scarborough Gallows Close		3.55 am		
H	(Q)	Maltby	4.05 am			
H		Bridlington		4.25 am		
H		Colwick		4.30 am		
H	MX	Sheffield	4.45 am			
H	MO	Stainforth & Hatfield		4.45 am		
E Unbraked	SX	Leeds Neville Hill		5.00 am		
H		Goole LMR		5.40 am		
H	(Q)	Bullcroft or Firbeck Colliery	5.45 am			
K		Selby		6.15 am		
H	SX	Crewe		6.20 am		
H	SX	Colwick		7.10 am		
K	TThSO	Hornsea Bridge		7.30 am		
K	SX	Withernsea		7.50 am		
H	MSX	York Yard via Gascoigne W.		7.55 am		
H		Doncaster Decoy		8.30 am		
K		Staddlethorpe		8.35 am		
F	MSX	Newport via Gascoigne W.		9.40 am		
E Unbraked	MO	York Skelton New Sidings via Gascoigne Wood	9.45 am			
H		Mottram		9.55 am		
K	SX	Market Weighton		10.30 am		
K	SO	Market Weighton		10.45 am		
E Unbraked	SX	York Skelton New Sidings via Gascoigne Wood	11.10 am			
C Fish	SX	Banbury		1.00 pm		
C Fish	SX	Leeds City		1.15 pm		
H	SO	Doncaster Decoy		1.20 pm		
H		Goole LMR		1.40 pm		
E Unbraked	SX	Leeds Neville Hill		2.05 pm		
C Fish		London King's Cross		2.55 pm		
H		York Yard S. via Gas. W.		3.00 pm		
H		Whitemoor		3.30 pm		
C Fish		East Goods Yard		3.40 pm		
C Fish		Guide Bridge		5.35 pm		
C Fish		Leeds City		6.20 pm		
C		York Dringhouses via Gascoigne Wood		6.27 pm		
C Fish	SO	York via Beverley		6.40 pm		
C Fish		Banbury		6.45 pm		
C Fish		East Goods Yard		6.55 pm		
H	ThX	Colwick	6.55 pm			
H	ThO	Annesley	6.55 pm			
C Fish		Normanton		7.40 pm		
H		Goole LMR		7.45 pm		
H	(Q)	Ickles	7.50 pm			
C Fish	SX	York via Beverley		8.00 pm		
C Fish	MO(Q)			(9.00 pm)	Paragon	8.40 pm
C		East Goods Yard		8.50 pm		
C Fish	MSX(Q)	Milford		9.00 pm		
C Fish	MO(Q)	Doncaster Old Yard			Paragon	9.20 pm
H		Goole LMR		9.20 pm		
H	FX	Annesley		9.45 pm		
C		Colwick		9.55 pm		
H		Doncaster Decoy		10.00 pm		
E Unbraked		Leeds Neville Hill		10.10 pm		
E Braked		Mottram		10.55 pm		
H		Sheffield	11.00 pm			
H		Bradford Adolphus Street		11.25 pm		
H	SO	Lincoln Pyewipe Junction		11.30 pm		
H	SX	Sheffield		11.30 pm		
H		Mexborough Top Yard		11.45 pm		

SUNDAYS

Class	Day(s) Run	Destination	Hull Mineral dep.	Hull Goods dep.	Hull other Location	depart
H		Sheffield		12.05 am		
H		York Yard S. via Gas. W.		12.10 am		
H		Selby		1.00 am		
H		Croft Junction via Gas. W.		1.20 am		
F		Newport via Gascoigne W.		7.15 am		

HULL FREIGHT TRAIN DEPARTURES (14th May to 30th September 1979)

Class	Day(s) Run	Destination	Hull Mineral dep.	Hull Goods dep.	Hull other Location	Depart
8D67	MX	Doncaster Decoy			New Yard	1.55 am
6V14	MThO	Baglan Bay			New Yard	8.58 am
6M30	TThSO	Rylstone			Dairycoates	12.25 pm
6M66	SX	Willesden			New Yard	4.00 pm
4L68	SX	Leeds			Freightliner Terminal	6.31 pm
7L64	SX	York			New Yard	6.55 pm
7J03	SX	Tinsley yard			New Yard	9.12 pm
7L82	SX	Healey Mills			New Yard	9.45 pm
6M55	MWFO	Rylstone			Dairycoates	10.30 pm

HULL FREIGHT TRAIN DEPARTURES (28th September 1992 to 16th May 1993)

Class	Day(s) Run	Destination	Hull Mineral dep.	Hull Goods dep.	Hull other Location	Depart
6V14	MWFO	Baglan Bay			Saltend B.P.	8.08 am
4N50	TThO	Wilton Freightliner Terminal			King George V Dock	8.18 am
6M30	MTThO	Rylstone			Dairycoates	5.40 pm
6M30	FO	Skipton Up Sidings			Dairycoates	5.40 pm
6M62	TThO	Ellesmere Port			Saltend B.P.	8.05 pm
6M88	MWFO	Spondon Courtaulds			Saltend B.P.	8.05 pm
			SUNDAYS			
6M62		Ellesmere Port			Saltend B.P.	5.53 pm

Abbreviations: **FO** - Fridays Only; **FX** - Fridays Excepted; **MFX** - Mondays and Fridays Excepted; **MO** - Mondays Only; **MSX** - Mondays and Saturdays Excepted; **MTThO** - Mondays, Tuesdays and Thursdays Only; **MThO** - Mondays and Thursdays Only; **MWFO** - Mondays, Wednesdays and Fridays Only; **MWThO** - Mondays, Wednesdays and Thursdays Only; **MX** - Mondays Excepted; **SO** - Saturdays Only; **SX** - Saturdays Excepted; **TFO** - Tuesdays and Fridays Only; **TO** Tuesdays Only; **TX** - Tuesdays excepted; **TThO** - Tuesdays and Thursdays Only; **TThSO** - Tuesdays, Thursdays and Saturdays Only; **ThO** - Thursdays Only; **ThX** - Thursdays Excepted.

SUMMARY OF NUMBER OF FREIGHT TRAIN DEPARTURES (including 'Q' paths)

Period	Monday	Tuesday	Wednesday	Thursdays	Friday	Saturday	Sunday	Totals
Summer 1927	105	119	118	119	117	110	2	**690**
Summer 1952	50	56	55	56	54	45	5	**321**
Summer 1979	7	7	7	8	7	2	0	**38**
Winter 1992	3	3	2	3	3	0	1	**15**

King's Cross allocated 61075 moves out of the Fish Sidings, Outward Yard with the 4.10 p.m. London fish train on 26th February 1963. Shortly after this date this train was put into the care of Dairycoates based B1's. *Peter Rose.*

In December 1935 the LNER opened a large new marshalling yard at Hessle to accept inbound freight traffic for the Hull area, including Hornsea and Withernsea. There were of course already a number of large yards within the city boundary, laid down and enlarged during the days of the North Eastern Railway and its younger neighbour, the Hull & Barnsley Railway. This new yard, which became known as Inwards Yard, was different from all the other 'flat' yards in that it was 'fully mechanised' with a hump and a control tower.

The LNER had, just a few years earlier, brought into operation their first fully mechanised yard at Whitemoor in Cambridgeshire to speed up the flow of freight traffic into London and the eastern counties from the industrial north. Having proved its worth to the LNER authorities, the 'mechanised yard' principle was to spread and Hull Inwards Yard was chosen as the next to be built.

Inwards Yard comprised, from west to east, six reception roads, thirty sorting sidings and four departure roads. The ten miles of sidings within the yard could hold over 2,100 wagons and up to 1,000 wagons could be dealt with in each of three shifts. Most traffic arrived from the west, leaving the main line to enter the yard complex at Hessle Haven but, trains arriving from an easterly direction could also be handled as they could be accomodated on the two most southerly reception roads. Once on a 'reception road', the train engine would be released and a shunting engine would push the train over the hump and 'cuts' of wagons (the 'cut' being a number of wagons bound for the same destination) would pass over the retarders and into the chosen siding. Once enough wagons had been assembled on any particular siding, they would be moved to a departure siding where a train engine would couple on, a brakevan having been attached to the rear of the train, and the train depart for its destination.

That is basically how Inward Yard worked but for a more intimate overview of its workings I have been given this description by Bert Worsfold who worked in the yard during the late 1950's.

"I first worked Inward Yard in the late 50's, as a 'chaser' and when today I see joggers and keep-fit fanatics using their spare time and possible spare money trying to keep themselves fit, I remember those days when we actually got paid to run and walk many miles in an eight hour shift, and kept fit for nothing.

After working at the older yards like Outward, with its gas lighting and not particularly good track layout (evenings at the west end of Outward, with all the fish and braked goods trains being marshalled and got away, could be hell on earth particularly on a foggy night), Inward was an oasis of calm and efficiency. At the east or outgoing end of the yard was an inspector and two shunters with their pilot engine, at one time an N8 0-6-2 tank and in latter years a 350 h.p. diesel shunter. Their job was to make up trains for destinations east of Hull - Bridlington, Scarborough, the daily pick-up goods for Hornsea and Withernsea, as well as the pilot and trip workings to Alexandra and King George docks.

At the other end of the yard, stretching right down to Hessle Haven signal box, was the entrance to the reception sidings with engine release road for the Hump Pilot and a short siding with a water column. When a train arrived on a reception line - the engine would after release travel down the engine road on the north side of the yard to Dairycoates shed - the cut card man, armed with a card sheet and pencil, together with shunting pole, would then examine the ticket and destination on each wagon or group of wagons. He also had a young assistant who would ride up and down on the pilot engine and take completed cut cards to the inspector at the top of the hump. The cut card man's job was most important as he had to know which road each destination needed to be and, any mistake on his part would mean the pilot engine having to go down the hump and bring out the wrong shunt and place it on its correct road. The cut card meanwhile would be transmitted by compressed air tube to the control tower, which controlled the retarders and points leading into the sorting sidings. The card would read something like 2 - 17. 6 - 5 (2 wagons for 17 road, 6 for 5 road etc.). The reception sidings were on a high embankment entirely open to the breezes, or at times howling gales, coming off the Humber, so the card man's job was not always as pleasant as it seemed. Once the cut card was in the control tower shunting could commence. The motive power was originally always a T1 4-8-0 tank or an A7 4-6-2 tank, Dairycoates having several of these huge engines for hump working at both Inward and Outward yards. Later the 350 h.p. diesel electric 0-6-0 shunters took over the job.

Colour light signals were used to control the hump shunting; green aspect to commence; yellow as the train approached the hump and red if progress was too fast. This signal was controlled by the Hump Top Inspector.

The hump driver's job was, to put it mildly, boring. You could only push a train at walking pace, and this went on all day. Sometimes all receptions were full and trains even stood out on the main line waiting to come in. At other times the reception roads would be empty but not for long as another train would come on. It was like a treadmill.

There were three chaser's on each shift at Inward and three shifts (0600, 1400, 2200) covered each twenty four hour period. As soon as the first wagon approached the hump top the chaser's job began. We had a small lobby op-

The reception roads at Inwards Yard, looking towards Hessle Haven 22nd January 1963.
Peter Rose.

posite the control tower and with windows in three sides of the lobby we could see all around. A tannoy system, with speakers on tall posts, operated all over the yard and would be used by the inspector or the controller in the tower. "On the top", was our signal to come out of the warmth of the little lobby, grab a brake stick and position ourselves near the four retarders. Goods wagons seemed to have minds of their own, some would slow down nicely as they hit the jaws of the retarder, others would scoot through and that's when we had to chase after them and brake them down. "Through the retarder!" meant a wagon or rake of wagons had somehow missed proper slowing down and would be hurtling down the yard. It was then you ran alongside, brake stick in left hand, grab the hand brake lever with your right hand and wedge the brake stick between the brake lever arm and spring, press hard down, and with one hand on the stick and the other on the brake handle, lift your feet and ride along exerting your body weight on the brake. Sometimes however they came too fast to catch and you could only flick down as many brakes as you could with your brake stick, and wait for the crash as they hit other wagons in the road. In the event of the road being empty, 'rail skates' (wedges) were placed on the tracks near the end so that wagons could not overrun the siding and foul the points at the East End. A 'Skate man' was employed at the east end to return the skate after any train had left the road. Inward was the only yard in Hull to use them and on entering a road at the East End, the shunter or guard had to remember to remove them. At Outward Yard the brakes of the end wagon on any siding were pinned down and on empty sidings a chaser rode down on the side of the first wagon, hanging on with a brake stick jammed in the underframe gear - securing the wagon he then walked back to the hump. At Inward we did not have to employ this rather dangerous practice.

Some wagons of course could not be retarded and coaching stock such as parcels vans had to be brought down by one of the chasers using the internal handbrake. Tank wagons were barred owing to the fire risk from sparks, and at that time we still had some vehicles such as milk or parcels vans with wooden wheel centres which were barred.

As the end of a train finally approached the hump top we would hear "Up for the Brake!", and after a brief argument as to who's turn it was to walk up to the top, a chaser would bring the brakevan down on the hand brake. We then had a break of around ten minutes whilst the pilot ran round another train and suddenly "On the top" would summon us out once again.

I left Inward Yard in July 1960 and although it was in many ways a dangerous job, all shunter's are exposed to danger, I cannot remember any serious accidents taking place. We were a happy gang and our Inspector, Harold Malton, was an experienced and dedicated railwayman, always ready to give help or advice, he was well liked and respected by everyone who knew him. In March 1974 Inward Yard closed after just 39 years and in doing so marked the end of an era and probably the end of BR as we knew it."

INWARD YARD SIDING ALLOCATION 1957

1	Fish empties.
2	Fish empties.
3	Bolsters.
4	Common users.
5	Common users.
6	Vans.
7	Vanfits.
8	Chalk Lane.
9	Fish kits, Goods, South Side, St Andrews Dock.
10	Outward yard.
11	H&B traffic for Neptune St and Springhead.
12	Hull.
13	New Yards and Shipping.
14	Spare.
15	Salt End tanks.
16	Wilmington.
17	Drypool.
18	Stepney.
19	King George Dock
20	Alexandra Dock.
21	Shops.
22	Coal for Mineral Yard.
23	Coal empties.
24	Beverley.
25	Hornsea.
26	Paragon.
27	Driffield.
28	Stations: Nafferton to Carnaby inc, Bridlington, Bankers and Scarborough.
29	Ideal Boilers & Radiators.
30	Withernsea.

On New Year's Day 1968 BR opened the Hull Freightliner terminal on the site once occupied by Priory Yard. Consisting of three rail tracks alongside a concrete hard standing wide enough to accomodate a three-lane road, the new terminal had sufficient land area on its north side to expand if traffic demanded.

The initial Freighliner service was an evening train to London Stratford terminal and additional services to other destinations such as Birmingham, Liverpool and Newcastle were planned as the Freightliner network expanded. The potential of the Hull terminal was promising to say the least; deep-sea container traffic was growing and being Britain's third seaport, Hull could have become a major gateway for overseas container business. However traffic levels never really approached those envisaged by the 1960's planners. The impact of the motorway system and labour disputes in the docks put paid to any plans the Dock's authority might have had of expanding the port facilities like those further down the East Coast at Felistowe. In 1987 what container traffic remained was transferred to the Leeds Freightliner terminal and the Hull yard was dismantled. For a time Speedlink services were run from the site but these too have gone the way of the wagonload traffic which once carried millions of tons to and from Hull.

To finish off this chapter of Hull's railway history we present a small selection of photographs showing the days when the diesels took over from steam and when freight trains were still in abundance in the city.

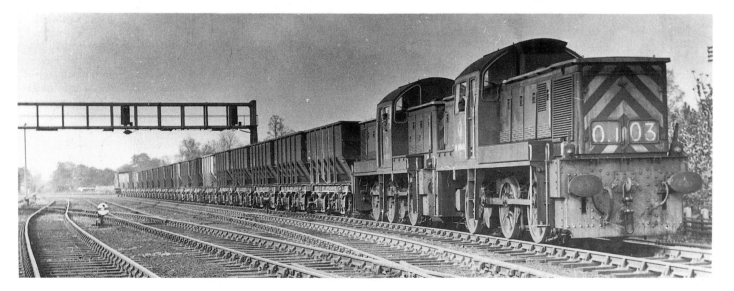

By the date of this picture steam traction in Hull was almost history, and nearly all the local trips had been turned over to diesel haulage. To accelerate the withdrawal of steam power, at one time or another a total of 33 of these Type 1 0-6-0 diesel hydraulic locomotives were working from Dairycoates shed. The design had originated on the Western Region, and all 56 engines were built at the Swindon works of the former Great Western Railway. D9548 the subject of our picture was new in July 1965, and first allocated to Cardiff Canton shed until 18th January 1967 when it joined the Dairycoates allocation of this largely unsuccessful class. It was destined to remain there until 18th January 1968 when it was condemned, even so this must have been more a case of "Surplus to Requirements" than "Beyond Economical Repair" for in the November of the same year it was sold off to industry to became the property of Messrs Stewart & Lloyds for use at their Corby steelworks. Here D9548, on 1st May 1967, is rather unusually working as a single unit passing under the Anlaby Road flyover at the head of the daily Hull to Bridlington goods trip. This kind of work was the origin for these engines but by the time they appeared in traffic such jobs had largely disappeared. Apart from displaying the trip number 8K11, the engine also exhibits the traditional single headlight of the steam era, and close examination further reveals the by now almost redundant 'fireman' still wearing his "greasetop hat".
The Rev.David Benson.

(previous page) **Two Type 1 0-6-0 diesel hydraulic locomotives blacken the sky whilst providing the head-end power for this Hessle Quarry to Earles Wilmington cement works chalk train in May 1967. Since before the "Great War" these workings had been quite literally an everyday occurrence, and at times of peak production it was not unknown for them to run on Bank Holidays, and if need be on Christmas Day. Previous generations of train watchers had been fortunate to witness more spectacular forms of motive power and in the 1930's it was not uncommon to see one of the large ex NER Class T1 4-8-0 tank engines on this job, and for many years it provided suitable employment for Dairycoates allocation of Raven Class A7 "Pacific" tank engines. Then finally after their demise in December 1957, and for the last decade of steam working, the same shed's WD 2-8-0s had an almost total monopoly on what the local railwaymen often referred to as the "Quarry Pilot". The front engine is D9551 whilst the train engine is D9523, and both are manned, a clear indication that tandem, not multiple working is in operation. The front engine is without headlamps, and once more shows a partly incorrect 0J03 headcode. The train is seen close to the junction of the Up Victoria Dock Line and the Up Main line at Botanic Gardens.**
The Rev.David Benson.

(left) **Reputed to be one of the last steam hauled block oil train from Saltend negotiates the goods lines at King George Dock in the Spring of 1967. Our old friend WD 90695 is in charge as two diesel hydraulics go the other way with a mixed goods train.**
The Rev. David Benson.